STORIES OF LIFE

JANET M. SANDERS

ISBN 979-8-88644-341-7 (Paperback)
ISBN 979-8-88644-344-8 (Digital)

Scripture taken from the NEW AMERICAN STANDARD BIBLE®, Copyright ©1960, 1962, 1963, 1968, 1971, 1972, 1973, 1975, 1977, 1995 by The Lockman Foundation. Used by permission. www.Lockman.org

Scripture taken from the NEW AMERICAN STANDARD BIBLE®, Copyright© 1960, 1962, 1963, 1968, 1971, 1972, 1973, 1975, 1977, 1995, 2020 by The Lockman Foundation. Used by permission.

Scripture taken from THE MESSAGE. Copyright© 1993, 1994, 1995, 1996, 2000, 2001, 2002. Used by permission of NavPress Publishing Group.

Scripture quotations taken from the Amplified Bible, Copyright© 1954, 1958, 1962, 1964. 1965, 1987 by The Lockman Foundation. Used by permission. (www.Lockman.org)

Artwork created by Riley Frere

Covenant Books
11661 Hwy 707
Murrells Inlet, SC 29576
www.covenantbooks.com

CONTENTS

INTRODUCTION

The Bible instructs us to share our story to help our families and future generations learn about the goodness of God and His love for us. This is my effort to fulfill that command.

> *Always giving thanks **for** all things in the name of our Lord Jesus Christ to God, even the Father. (Ephesians 5:20 NASB 1995; emphasis mine)*

> *In everything give thanks; for this is God's will for you in Christ Jesus. (1 Thessalonians 5:18 NASB 1995)*

That little word *for* has been the source of much discussion and interpretation. Am I to thank God for all the evil that has happened? I don't think so. God is love. He is the God of love. He is for me, not against me. At the same time, He does correct us and show us a better path to take. The Holy Spirit is always trying to nudge us into going the better way.

What God is saying to me in these verses is, "Look at the bigger picture, be thankful that I have walked with you through all the difficulties, be thankful you have learned and matured as a result of the difficulties."

I am not to be thankful that bad happened but that I was able to learn from it. Some people can learn just by listening to the consequences another person suffered. Other people, like me, need to suffer those consequences before they learn. God would rather we learn from listening to Him and believing Him (trust and obey). But we are to be thankful no matter how we learn because the ultimate goal is to mature spiritually as Ephesians states,

> *Until we all attain to the unity of the faith, and of the knowledge of the Son of God, to a mature man, to the measure of the stature which belongs to the fullness of Christ. (Ephesians 4:13 NASB 1995)*

My desire for this book is that it be a handy reference book of encouragement. If God will do it for one person, He will do it for anyone. God is not a respecter of persons. He is a loving, caring God, but He is also a Father that expects respect, obedience, and believing in Him. Trust and obey and God will always come through for you. Learn from the mistakes of others so you don't fall into the same snares.

He has never failed me. He has also never failed to solve a problem in a better way than I was asking or hoping for. We think, *If God will just do this…*, but if we let Him, He will do *that* instead, and it will be so much better in the long run.

> *Now to Him who is able to do far more abundantly beyond all that we ask or think, according to the power that works within us. (Ephesians 3:20 NASB 1995)*

Accept and believe that He is working on your behalf. Eventually you will see that His way was working for your good, and the result will be so very much better than you had thought it could be. It takes time, but after a while, when you can look back, you will see how God's way was so very much better and how far you have come because you trusted Him. Then you can share your story with others as Psalms 78 instructs.

> *Listen, O my people, to my instruction; incline your ears to the words of my mouth. I will open my mouth in a parable; I will utter dark sayings*

of old, which we have heard and known, and our fathers have told us. We will not conceal them from their children, but tell to the generation to come the praises of the Lord, and His strength and His wondrous works that He has done. For He established a testimony in Jacob and appointed a law in Israel, which He commanded our fathers that they should teach them to their children, that the generation to come might know, even the children yet to be born, that they may arise and tell them to their children, that they should put their confidence in God and not forget the works of God but keep His commandments. (Psalm 78:1–7 NASB 1995)

Historical Facts

These historical facts are to help the reader recognize and understand the differences our culture has gone through in just a short seventy years. A lot of what people see as totally normal and acceptable in today's society didn't even exist a few short decades ago. That isn't to say the past was wrong, and we have corrected it. That may be true in some areas, but in other areas, it is totally the opposite. We have lost greatly from where we were.

1940
HOLY
BIBLE

1940s

US population: 132,164,569

Number of states: 48

Average annual income in 1940 was $1,368 and in 1949 $2,950 (in today's dollars, approximately $24,500 and $31,100).

Average life expectancy was sixty years for men and sixty-eight for women.

Only 55 percent of all US homes had indoor plumbing at the start of the decade. That left 45 percent of the homes using outhouses, wells, and hauling water.

In 1940, 47 percent of the US population only had an eighth-grade education. Education was focused on reading, writing, arithmetic, and learning a trade. Reciting the Lord's Prayer and the Pledge of Allegiance were the beginning to each school day.

The Census Bureau reported 4.6 percent of adults held a bachelor's degree in 1940.

A gallon of gas cost an average of $0.11 at the start of the decade and $0.18 at its end.

A new car cost $850 in 1940 and $1,420 in 1949.

The USA was involved in WWII from December 7, 1941, when the Japanese bombed Pearl Harbor, Hawaii, until it ended with VE Day on May 8, 1945, and the Japanese surrender in September 1945.

The age to be drafted into the US military was lowered from twenty-one to eighteen in 1942.

Fifty countries signed the charter establishing the United Nations in 1945.

Captain America was introduced to the public by Marvel Comics in March 1941.

Charles Yeager broke the sound barrier on October 14, 1947, at Mach 1 at an altitude of forty-five thousand feet.

The NBA was founded in 1946.

Chicago Bears won four of the five Super Bowl games in which they played during the decade.

The New York Yankees won four of the five World Series games they played during the decade.

1950s

US population: 151,325,798

Number of States: 50

On January 3, 1959, Alaska became the forty-ninth state, and on August 21, 1959, Hawaii became the fiftieth state in the USA.

The baby boom peaked in 1957 when just under 4.3 million babies were born in the USA.

In the 1950s, if a girl was pregnant and not married, she was shunned by society and shipped off to some other location to have the baby and give it up for adoption. The male wasn't considered accountable. He was only sowing "wild oats."

Each school day was still started with the Pledge of Allegiance and the Lord's Prayer.

Average annual salary was $3,210 in 1950 and $5,010 by 1959 (in today's dollars, approximately $34,000 and $43,300).

Minimum wage was $0.75 an hour.

A loaf of white bread cost $0.12, and ten pounds of potatoes were $0.35.

Except for working as menial labor, men wore suits and women wore dresses.

Disposable diapers were invented over a long period of time and styles until Proctor & Gamble came out with a workable version in 1956—and all the mothers said, "Hooray!"

Interstate highways were started through the Federal-Aid Highway Act in 1956 to create forty-one thousand miles of national highways across the country.

A gallon of gas cost $0.18 at the beginning and $0.25 at the end of the decade.

The average cost of a new car was $1,510 in 1950 and $2,200 in 1959.

Otis had the first self-service elevator, and Xerox made the first photocopy machine.

CBS broadcast the first color television program on June 25, 1951.

Elvis Presley was introduced to radio listeners on July 8, 1953, with his song "That's All Right."

The first indoor mall was opened in Minnesota.

Fast food started when McDonald's franchised on April 15, 1955, and the first burgers sold for $0.15.

Rock and roll was a highlight of the 1950s culture.

Civil Rights became a focus during this decade. On May 17, 1954, the US Supreme Court ruled that separate schools for Black students were inherently unequal and unconstitutional. On December 1, 1955, Rosa Parks refused to give up her bus seat for a White passenger in Montgomery, Alabama. The vast majority of racial unrest was in the Southern states.

The Salk vaccine was created to eliminate the polio epidemic that killed 22 percent of the children that contracted the disease.

In 1957, the Asian flu **pandemic** killed over one million people, 116,000 in the US.

The first credit card was issued in the 1950s.

1960s

US population: 179,323,175
Number of states: 50
Nearly half of America's population was under eighteen years old.
Average family income was $5,600. For households headed by a person sixty-five years or older, the income was $2,900.

Average life expectancy in 1960 was 69.3 years (66.6 years for men and 73.1 for females).

A new house cost $16,500.

Minimum wage in 1969 was $1.60.

Over 90 percent of homes had at least one TV (only three channels were available—ABC, CBS, NBC).

About 98 percent of households in 1960 only had black and white TV due to the high cost of color which became available in 1954.

About 65 percent of Americans were churchgoers.

Average cost of a gallon of gasoline was $0.31.

FDA approved the world's first commercially produced birth control pill.

The St. Louis Gateway Arch was finished on October 28, 1965.

On February 9, 1964, the Beatles first performed before a US audience on *The Ed Sullivan Show*.

President John F. Kennedy was assassinated on November 22, 1963.

Neil Armstrong took the first step on the moon on July 20, 1969.

On October 1, 1962, James H. Meredith became the first Black student to attend the University of Mississippi, one of the reluctant states to accept Civil Rights changes.

Martin Luther King Jr. delivered his famous speech, "I Have a Dream," on August 28, 1963.

The 1960s were marked by the struggle for Civil Rights both for Blacks in the Southern states and women and minorities across the country. In 1964, President Johnson pushed a Civil Rights act through Congress that prohibited discrimination in public places against women and minorities and promised equal opportunities in the workplace to all. In a historically male-dominated and controlled work environment, for them to relinquish equal pay to women, whom they viewed as only people that belonged at home caring for the children, was a very slow process. In the South, the Blacks were coming out of the stigma of having been viewed only as illiterate slaves.

There were 3,711,000 farms in America, averaging about 303 acres apiece. Farmers made up 8.3 percent of the labor force.

1970s

US population: 203,302,031

The '70s had massive inflation, in part due to the energy crisis in the Middle East.

The Organization of Arab Petroleum Exporting Countries announced an embargo on oil exports to the US on October 15, 1973.

Average individual income was $9,350 at the beginning and by 1979 was $17,550.

A new house went from $23,400 to $58,500.

Five pounds of sugar cost $0.39.

A gallon of milk averaged $0.62, and a dozen eggs were $0.59.

In 1970, 34 percent of the US population had completed high school.

A gallon of gas rose from $0.36 to $0.86.

Average cost of a new car went from $3,900 to $5,770.

The first cell phone was in 1973 and weighed 4.4 pounds.

First personal computer was available in 1974.

Microsoft was founded in 1975 by Bill Gates and Paul Allen.

Apple Computer Company was created in 1976.

Before DVDs, Blu-ray, and personal video recorders, there were VCRs. In 1970, Philips made a home video cassette format. For the first time, people could record a television show and watch it at a time of their choosing instead of having to watch the live viewing. As a bonus, they could fast-forward through commercials or rewind with the VCR technology.

In 1972, Congress approved the Equal Rights Amendment, stating that equal rights could not be denied to anyone based on their sex.

In 1979, women only earned 62 percent as compared to their male counterparts for doing the same work.

On January 22, 1973, the Supreme Court legalized abortion in the case of Roe v. Wade.

President Richard M. Nixon resigned from office on August 8, 1974.

The last Americans departed Vietnam on April 30, 1975.

Fashion in the '70s saw bell-bottom pants, flowing maxi dresses, as well as miniskirts and short shorts. Platform shoes with soles between two to four inches thick were worn by both men and women.

These were tumultuous years where groups fought for equality, students protested the Vietnam war, and the digital revolution began.

1980s

US population: 226,542,199

US entered the biggest economic downturn since the Great Depression. The prime rate reached a record high of 21.5 percent.

Inflation hovered between 6.51 percent and 13.91 percent, and unemployment reached 8 percent.

The stock market lost 22.6 percent of its value on Black Monday, October 19, 1987.

Average annual income was $19,500.

Minimum wage in 1980 was $3.10.

The average home cost was $92,800.

A gallon of milk cost $2.16, and eggs were $0.83 a dozen.

Candy bars cost $0.25.

A first-class stamp cost $0.15 in 1980 and $0.25 in 1988.

A gallon of gas averaged $1.19.

Seat belts were legally required to be used starting in 1984 even though they had been installed in cars since 1968.

The AIDS **pandemic** started in 1981 and is still active. It has killed thirty-five million people.

Cable TV was available for a price. Those without cable still only received three channels: ABC, CBS, and NBC.

Twenty-four-hour news programming on cable TV was started by Ted Turner on June 1, 1981.

By the end of the '80s, 60 percent of television owners had cable service. The most revolutionary cable network was MTV, which debuted August 1, 1981.

The original consumer CD player was put on the market by Sony in 1982.

The first analog cellular phone system became available to Americans in 1983. There were thousands of people on the waiting list. It could only store thirty numbers, and charging took ten hours with thirty minutes of talk time. It weighed two pounds and cost $3,995.

Apple launched its Macintosh computer in 1984.

Americans embraced a new conservatism in social, economic, and political life during the 1980s, characterized by President Ronald Reagan. To Reagan's credit, he had numerous fiscal policy successes, such as cutting the top individual tax rate from 70 percent to 28 percent and the corporate rate from 46 percent to 34 percent. On spending, Reagan's original February 1981 plan proposed enough cuts to bring outlays down to 19.3 percent of GDP by 1984 and balance the budget. With a Congress unwilling to make serious cuts, the deficit remained high, and spending was stuck at over 22 percent until the late 1980s.

Game
Over

1990s

US population: 248,709,873

Yearly inflation rate was 5.39 percent in 1990.

Life expectancy in the US had risen to 75.4 years. There were 250,437 Americans who were ninety-five years old or older.

Minimum wage for most of the decade was $4.25.

The average family income in 1995 was $40,611 up from $28,960 in 1990.

Five pounds of potatoes cost $0.89, Coca-Cola cost $1.99 for an eight-pack.

Eggs cost $0.89 a dozen.

A General Electric washing machine cost $199.

A gallon of gas remained around $1.30 for the decade.

The average cost of a new car was $9,437 to $13,600.

To get online, you had to use dial-up or Netscape.

At the height of their popularity in 1994, sixty-one million people used pagers.

The Sony PlayStation was released in 1995.

Microsoft released Windows 3.0.

The Dow Jones Industrial Average closed above ten thousand for the first time on March 29, 1999.

On August 2, 1990, the Iraqi army invaded Kuwait. When negotiations failed, the United States and thirty-nine other countries launched military forces and attacked the Iraqi Army in January 1991 and officially liberated Kuwait on February 25, 1991.

David Dinkins was sworn in as the first African-American mayor of New York City.

The college entry rate for young Blacks was 57.5 percent in 1990.

In 1995, 25 percent of the US population had completed one to three years of college.

Women's wages had increased to 72 percent of their male counterparts by 1990.

2000s

US population: 281,421,906

Inflation was 3.36 percent and unemployment around 4 percent.

Minimum wage increased to $5.85 in 2007 and $7.25 in 2009.

The average yearly income was $40,373.

The median cost of a new home was $119,600.

A dozen eggs cost $0.89 and five pounds of potatoes were $0.79.

A first-class stamp cost $0.34.

A gallon of gas cost $1.26.

Average price of a new vehicle in 2000 was $21,850.

On September 11, 2001, hijacked airliners crashed into the World Trade Center, the Pentagon, and a field in Shanksville, Pennsylvania.

War was waged by the US and Britain against Iraq on March 19, 2003. In 2004, the US returned sovereignty to an interim government in Iraq.

Hurricane Katrina, the costliest hurricane in US history at that time, hit southeast Louisiana on August 29, 2005.

Apple Computer, Inc. unveiled the first iPod on October 23, 2001.

In 2000, White women earned 74.7 percent as much as White men did for the same work. Black women's earnings were 85.2 percent of Black men's, and Hispanic women made 87.7 percent as much as did Hispanic men.

The swine flu **pandemic** in 2009 primarily affected children and young adults under sixty-five years old. According to the CDC, 80 percent of the deaths were under sixty-five years old. This is unusual, since most strains of flu virus cause more death in the elderly. In this case, the older adults seemed to have built up enough natural immunity over time and weren't affected as much. Approximately 1.4 billion people were infected with up to 575,400 deaths, which is a death toll of .0004 percent.

2010

2010s

US population: 308,745,538

Unemployment in 2010 was 9.5 percent and dropped steadily to 3.7 percent in 2019.

Inflation was 1.64 percent.

Prime rate was 3.25 percent.

Average family income was $49,445.

The US Census Bureau reported that the percentage of Americans living below the poverty line ($10,830 for an individual and $22,050 for a family of four) reached a fifteen-year high in 2010. That year, an estimated forty-four million people, or 14.3 percent of the US population, were living in poverty.

The median cost of a new home was $221,800 in 2010 and $302,400 in 2018.

The US Census Bureau reported 33.4 percent of the adult US population had a bachelor's degree or higher on March 30, 2017.

In general, the American society now not only accept single parents for any reason, they also accept homosexuals and transgender people. The morals and value system in the country has drastically changed over the past sixty years.

A gallon of gas averaged $2.96.

In 2010, a new Buick Regal cost $25,245, a Chrysler Town & Country was $17,750, and a Ford Fusion cost $19,695.

Women earned 82.3 percent compared to their male counterparts in 2019.

The decade was plagued with school shootings, terrorist attacks, riots, and general civil unrest.

On November 2, 2016, the Chicago Cubs won their first World Series since 1908.

HOW I KNOW GOD EXISTS

Encounters

A.   Encounter #1 (4 Years Old)

In 1948, my parents sold their home in town and purchased a farmhouse on five acres in the country in search of a more wholesome environment for their family. This property was on a dirt road, half mile either direction to a cross street, with open farmland across the road owned by a large farm whose home was closer to the cross street to the north. There were a few other country homes with acreage on this mile-long stretch of road in the area south of Detroit, Michigan, referred to as the downriver area.

The farmhouse my parents purchased was just a shell. The basement, outside frame, first-story studs were in place, along with a small section of flooring in the back of the house. The rest of the flooring, walls, plumbing, electrical, etc. all needed to be finished. My parents planned to do the work themselves.

The following year(s), as my parents and my eleven-year-old brother worked on creating a farm and finishing the interior construction of the farmhouse, I, now four years old, was continuously sent off to play away from the work area.

It was a sunny day in late spring when I discovered turning the homemade picnic bench upside down made a great play boat with its high ends and was just wide enough for me to sit inside. Many a day I floated down my imaginary river in my makeshift boat listening to Kate Smith sing "Shine On, Harvest Moon" playing on the radio coming from the open kitchen window.

One day, as I peacefully sat there smelling the beautiful fragrance of my mom's lilac bush that was in bloom in the front yard, I started noticing the trees that lined the side of our property. Their leaves were different shapes on different trees, the shades of green varied on the multiple types of trees growing there. I remembered how dead they had all been during the winter, and when the leaves grew back, they didn't get mixed up. The elm, oak, maple, redwood, and pine trees all knew which shape of leaf was specifically theirs. They came back as the same tree they had been.

Then I thought about the warm sunshine, the blue skies above, and the fluffy white clouds—how the seasons had changed and come back again. I thought about how the moon comes up at night and the warm breezes during the day.

It is all so organized, so controlled, there has to be someone up there that makes it all work. It couldn't be by accident. There is too much care, organization, control to the system, I thought to myself.

I said to the Creator of it all, "I am just a little kid right now, but someday I want to get to know you." At that moment, I heard singing and I knew there is more than one up there. As I understand now, they were the angels singing that I heard.

It was an experience I have never forgotten and one I am very thankful for. As much as I didn't understand about the Bible and its teaching growing up, at least I KNEW there is a God in heaven. There was never a question in my mind about that no matter what people said.

> *In the beginning God created the heavens and the earth. And the earth was a formless and desolate emptiness, and darkness was over the surface of the deep, and the Spirit of God was hovering over the surface of the waters. Then God said, "Let there be light"; and there was light. God saw that the light was good; and God separated the light from the darkness. God called the light "day," and the darkness He called "night." And there was evening and there was morning, one day.*

Then God said, "Let there be an expanse in the midst of the waters, and let it separate the waters from the waters." God made the expanse, and separated the waters that were below the expanse from the waters that were above the expanse; and it was so. God called the expanse "heaven." And there was evening and there was morning, a second day.

Then God said, "Let the waters below the heavens be gathered into one place, and let the dry land appear"; and it was so. And God called the dry land "earth," and the gathering of the waters He called "seas"; and God saw that it was good. Then God said, "Let the earth sprout vegetation, plants yielding seed, and fruit trees on the earth bearing fruit according to their kind with seed in them"; and it was so. The earth produced vegetation, plants yielding seed according to their kind, and trees bearing fruit with seed in them, according to their kind; and God saw that it was good. And there was evening and there was morning, a third day.

Then God said, "Let there be lights in the expanse of the heavens to separate the day from the night, and they shall serve as signs and for seasons, and for days and years; and they shall serve as lights in the expanse of the heavens to give light on the earth"; and it was so. God made the two great lights, the greater light to govern the day, and the lesser light to govern the night; He made the stars also. God placed them in the expanse of the heavens to give light on the earth, and to govern the day and the night, and to separate the light from the darkness; and God saw that it was good. And there was evening and there was morning, a fourth day.

Then God said, "Let the waters teem with swarms of living creatures, and let birds fly above the earth in the open expanse of the heavens." And

God created the great sea creatures and every living creature that moves, with which the waters swarmed, according to their kind, and every winged bird according to its kind; and God saw that it was good. God blessed them, saying, "Be fruitful and multiply, and fill the waters in the seas, and let birds multiply on the earth." And there was evening and there was morning, a fifth day.

Then God said, "Let the earth produce living creatures according to their kind: livestock and crawling things and animals of the earth according to their kind"; and it was so. God made the animals of the earth according to their kind, and the livestock according to their kind, and everything that crawls on the ground according to its kind; and God saw that it was good.

Then God said, "Let Us make mankind in Our image, according to Our likeness; and let them rule over the fish of the sea and over the birds of the sky and over the livestock and over all the earth, and over every crawling thing that crawls on the earth." So God created man in His own image, in the image of God He created him; male and female He created them. God blessed them; and God said to them, "Be fruitful and multiply, and fill the earth, and subdue it; and rule over the fish of the sea and over the birds of the sky and over every living thing that moves on the earth."

Then God said, "Behold, I have given you every plant yielding seed that is on the surface of all the earth, and every tree which has fruit yielding seed; it shall be food for you; and to every animal of the earth and to every bird of the sky and to everything that moves on the earth which has life, I have given every green plant for food"; and it was so. And God saw all that He had made, and behold, it was very good. And there was evening and there was morning, the sixth day. (Genesis 1:1–31 NASB)

Can you see how organized God was in the creation of the world?

B.   Encounter #2 (33 Years Old)

While I was working as a secretary in the offices of a manufacturing business in Bradenton, Florida, a new girl, Vivian, that had just gotten married and moved to Florida from New Jersey was hired. Her office was down the hall a few doors from mine. Some of the office girls occasionally congregated at lunch in my office to visit and share news. My contribution was to sit quietly, listening and knitting.

After lunch on Wednesday, June 14, 1978, Vivian asked me to come to her office. When I arrived, she had a gift for me. She said, "Jesus loves you just as you are," and handed me a Bible with my name engraved on it. She invited me to attend church with her that Friday night for the last night of a revival they were holding. I was so impressed to have been given such a wonderful gift (even though I couldn't believe Jesus cared about me) I accepted her invitation to church.

My twelve-year-old son, John, and I met Vivian and her husband, Chris, at their home for dinner that Friday evening and then proceeded to the church service.

It was a small church away from the main roads and surrounded by woods. I had been to a number of churches of different denominations searching for that God I knew existed from my four-year-old encounter. They all said the right things, but somehow I couldn't find that tangible proof I was seeking. I wanted something more than words.

I didn't know what I was looking for, but I knew when it wasn't there. A lot of people know God as Savior, and that is fine. It is the gateway to heaven. But my heart wanted something more. I wanted to know Him as Lord. I wanted God to be my close personal friend that could help me with life here and now and not just in the hereafter.

It was the end of the church service, and again it seemed this one was not any different than the rest of the churches I had visited. The pastor was giving his closing prayer, and I was standing impatiently, waiting for it to be over.

Then suddenly, a huge wind came from behind the pastor and knocked me unconscious, and I fell back into the pew. A tornado? A hurricane? Everything was swirling around in my mind. The pastor had been on the platform saying his final prayer, and when I regained consciousness, he had his hand on my forehead, praying. I heard people saying something in tongues (a language I didn't understand) and then someone saying in English, "A woman needs to come to the Lord." Slowly, I stood back up and knew I needed to go forward.

I was so terrified of retaliation from people at that time in my life (a result of PTSD) that I stood frozen, unable to break through the fear. Eventually, after the congregation had left (unbeknownst to me)—that is, everyone except us—I whispered to Vivian, "Will you go forward with me?" We walked, with my eyes shut, up the outside isle (so the people that weren't there couldn't see me) to the altar where the pastor led me in the Sinners Prayer as I responded in a whisper (to keep those people from hearing that I thought were still there). Years later, Vivian told me the Holy Spirit had let her know if I didn't come to the Lord that night, I would be dead within a week. Thus, she was going more than the extra mile dealing with this very strange-acting female.

On the drive home, I told the Lord if He was smart enough to write the Bible, then He was smart enough to teach me what it says. The next morning, when I opened the Bible Vivian had given me, it was alive! And it was talking to me! I could understand what I was reading and started seeing applications to my real-life situations.

It was so exciting I spent every waking moment I could reading my Bible and learning what it said. A whole new world full of hope and good things was opening up to me. The more I read and understood how it applied to me, the more I changed the way I believed, the way I acted, and the way I spoke. It has been forty-four years now, and that love for Jesus has never changed. The Bible still talks to me, and Jesus is still my life. I am nothing on my own. All the good that has been done in and through my life is because of Him.

These are the verses Vivian noted on the inside cover to dedicate my Bible and where I started:

> *But seek first His kingdom and His righteousness, and all these things will be added to you. (Matthew 6:33 NASB 1995)*

> *Trust in the Lord with all your heart and do not lean on your own understanding. In all your ways acknowledge Him, and He will make your paths straight. (Proverbs 3:5–6 NASB)*

> *Delight yourself in the Lord; And He will give you the desires of your heart. Commit your way to the Lord, Trust also in Him, and He will do it. (Psalm 37:4–5 NASB)*

> *The Lord is my shepherd, I shall not want. He makes me lie down in green pastures; He leads me beside quiet waters. He restores my soul; He guides me in the paths of righteousness for His name's sake. Even though I walk through the valley of the shadow of death I fear no evil, for You are with me; Your rod and Your staff, they comfort me. You prepare a table before me in the presence of my enemies; You have anointed my head with oil; My cup overflows. Surely goodness and loving kindness will follow me all the days of my life, and I will dwell in the house of the Lord forever. (Psalm 23 NASB 1995)*

How I Learned to Trust God

Trusting God

Trust in the Lord with all your heart and do not lean on your own understanding. In all your ways acknowledge Him, and He will make your paths straight. (Proverbs 3:5–6 NASB 1995)

Learning to trust God has continued to come in stages for me. First, for protection, then finances, and then it was little by little over the years with each situation he brought me through. Things didn't always go right, but I could always look back and see good had come from it.

A.   For Protection

I first learned to trust God as my protector in July 1978 as a brand-new Christian. My divorce from my second husband (a violent criminal personality that was very abusive and controlling) was made final on May thirty-first, two weeks before my second encounter with the Lord on June 16, 1978 (explained in detail above).

Because my husband had been out of the state for eight months and I didn't have contact with him or a current address for him, the divorce petition was posted in the newspaper and mailed to his last known address. The divorce was finalized without his direct knowledge. I was legally free, and the police would be able to help me now, but, he had to be told. I mailed the divorce papers to his mother's address, knowing she would be in contact with him eventually.

The day came, over a year later, when I got his phone call. He was in town, furious, and "coming to get me." Without it going through my mind, I said, "I have talked to the police." That was equal to throwing gasoline on a blazing fire. The Holy Spirit led those words because after being terrorized by him for ten years, there is no way those words went through my mind or would have ever come out of my mouth any other way. It wasn't a lie because actually I had talked to a police officer. But the conversation was one of courtesy and nothing at all about protection or him.

That evening, after the phone call, I sent my son to spend the night at a friend's house and I spent the entire night awake and waiting for the Molotov cocktail to come through my front window or some similar response from him. When it never happened, I realized somehow God had protected me.

Years later, I found out he had already picked up a load of illegal contraband before he called me, and when I mentioned talking to the police, he immediately left town. The same words I thought had signed my death certificate were the actual words that saved me because they sent him running.

> *Submit therefore to God, resist the devil and*
> *he will flee from you. (James 4:7 NASB 1995)*

> *Let your conversation be without covetousness*
> *and be content with such things as ye have for he*
> *hath said, I will never leave thee, nor forsake thee,*
> *So that we may boldly say, The Lord is my helper,*
> *and I will not fear what man shall do unto me.*
> *(Hebrews 13:5–6 KJV)*

God knew everything. The Holy Spirit directed my words and saved me when I was totally unaware. Trust God. He always has your best at heart and is on your side no matter what the circumstances look like.

If we only serve God half-heartedly, then we will not have confidence in Him to deliver us from trouble.

The devil is always on one side, whispering, "I am going to kill you." God is on the other side promising life and life abundantly. We are the deciding witness, standing in the middle. We decide whom we are going to trust in each situation all day long every day.

Do I trust God or trust myself, my friends, what the world says, etc.?

B. As Provider

In June 1978, when I committed my life to the Lord, I was thirty-three years old. I was working as a secretary for a few cents over minimum wage, which was about $2.65 an hour at that time. My son and I lived in a two-bedroom duplex in Bradenton, Florida.

Our funds were so limited we didn't use the heat or AC or any extras. We had just enough money to pay rent, electricity, water, basic food, and gas to and from work. No telephone or extra trips to the store, no little treats or snacks. We picked up aluminum cans along the roadway in walking distance and sold the metal for the only spending money we had.

My furniture was not only bargain basement; it was the stuff from out back in the dumpster. We used cement blocks and boards to make shelves. My pride and integrity wouldn't allow me to apply for welfare or borrow money whether on a credit card or loan and become what I viewed as a thief because I knew I couldn't pay it back. So we just did without the extras instead. We had a roof over our heads, food enough to live, and peace in our home. That was a far cry from where we had been and was such a blessing at that point in time. When you have been without something for a long time, even a little can generate great joy.

After a couple of weeks with the Lord, I heard the word *tithe*. I inquired about it from my mentor, Vivian, and found out it says in the Bible to give God 10 percent of your income. It is all His to begin with, and He only asks for a small part of it back to show our commitment to Him.

I was so thankful to have Him on my side I decided to do it. I didn't know how I would ever pay the bills at the end of that month, but for now, I was just going to be obedient. My logical mind said I would not have enough money, but somehow, to my amazement, as I wrote check after check, there actually was enough, and all the bills for that month were paid. A little bit lower cost here, a little unexpected credit there, and it all worked out.

By the middle of the next month, I received a call to start a new job that I had taken an application test for several months before. By then, I had given up on ever hearing from them. It was a government position with the USPS at over twice the pay and lots of benefits I never had before. To me, that was a concrete example of what happens when you trust God with money. Tithing was easy compared to the hellish existence I had been living before I committed to Jesus. Then once He showed me the results from tithing, I was committed for life.

Since then, there have been many times it LOOKED LIKE I didn't/ wouldn't/couldn't have enough money, but it always worked out that there was enough.

There was one month, August, I used to hate. After being a Christian for some twenty-one years, I had moved my business office from my home to a strip mall. With all the new furniture, equipment, and extra expenses, the first year was a financial loss. The second year, my total income for the month of August was $8. Yes, you heard correctly, $8 income for a business. The rent, utilities, phone, and employee wages all still had to be paid. Determined to not quit, I still tithed my whole $0.80, and somehow I was always able to pay the bills. Every year for many years, August would be an extremely low month on income. After that first time, I anticipated the downturn in income and was prepared for it.

> *Trust in the Lord with all your heart and do not lean on your own understanding. In all your ways acknowledge Him and He will make your paths straight. (Proverbs 3:5–6 NASB)*

God has proven that scripture to me so many times. As imperfect as I have always been, He has never failed me or failed to take care of me financially.

> *"Bring the whole tithe into the storehouse, so that there may be food in My house, and test Me now in this," says the Lord of hosts, "if I will not open for you the windows of heaven and pour out for you a blessing until it overflows. Then I will rebuke the devourer for you, so that it will not destroy the fruits of the ground; nor will your vine in the field cast its grapes," says the Lord of hosts. (Malachi 3:10 NASB 1995)*

This is the only place in the Bible I have ever found where God says we can test Him. He is so very faithful when it comes to finances.

C. With My Health (Situation #1)

I learned to trust God with my health on many occasions when minor things came up. Then a few times with not-so-minor issues.

In December 1990, while living in Bradenton, Florida, I traveled sixty miles to Tampa to attend a two-day tax seminar for my business and the upcoming tax season. The temperature in the conference room for these meetings is always set low, presumably to keep people awake. However, from the beginning, I became so cold I started shivering until it turned into shaking uncontrollably.

Not wanting to disrupt the meeting, I held tightly onto the chair seat to keep from falling off. At the first break of the morning, a little disoriented and unsteady on my feet, I left the conference room and headed to my car. Once there, I got behind the wheel to go home and realized I couldn't drive. I was dizzy, had limited vision, was still shaking, and knew my mind wasn't clear to recognize obstacles or other cars.

I didn't know what was wrong with me and just prayed and asked the Lord to somehow get me home. After resting for a few minutes, I drove the entire way home, only able to focus on things directly in front of me. It was sixty miles through heavy downtown highway and interstate traffic. God and His angels were definitely the ones guiding and directing that vehicle and who got me home safely that day.

Once home, there was a message on the answering machine from my daughter's school. She was sick in the nurse's office, and I needed to pick her up. Though all I wanted was to go to bed, I knew my day was long from over.

I had recuperated enough to call the doctor before leaving home and was told to bring my daughter, Angela, directly into their office. Angela checked out with just a virus that a prescription would cure.

While talking with the doctor, I mentioned the ordeal I had gone through that morning. The doctor ran an EKG on me and said I had had a heart attack and ordered me directly to the hospital immediately. I respectfully declined and said I just didn't feel good and wanted to go home.

Once home again, I stayed in bed for thirty-six hours, just getting worse, until I finally agreed to go to the hospital. I had all the symptoms of a heart attack, but I kept praying, "I am healed by Jesus's stripes."

By this point, I wasn't able to drive, so my father-in-law drove from town, picked me up, and took me to the hospital. After getting sick to my stomach in the emergency room, they rushed me back and started their barrage of tests.

The cardiologist at the hospital came in after reading all the test results they had been running on me and said, "What are you doing wasting my time?" He was quite blunt, didn't explain, and just released me. I was sick at home for a few more days, but it finally left. I never found out what illness was attacking me, but it didn't matter. God's promises of healing are solid and can be totally relied upon. When someone doesn't recover, I believe there were other factors we don't know or don't understand, but that doesn't change God's promises. What it means is that we don't know everything.

*Surely our griefs He himself bore, and our
sorrows He carried; Yet we ourselves esteemed*

*Him stricken, Smitten of God, and afflicted. But He was pierced through for our transgressions, He was crushed for our iniquities; the chastening for our well-being fell upon Him, and **by His scourging we are healed**. (Isaiah 53:4–5 NASB 1995; emphasis mine)*

D.   With My Health (Situation #2)

On April 3, 2013, I had a one hundred-percent blockage in a main artery to my heart that resulted in a heart attack. It was a Wednesday morning, and I hadn't been able to sleep much the night before. About one o'clock that previous night, I awoke and started getting up, taking aspirin every couple hours, each time hoping I would be able to get back to sleep. It was always my *thing* to take two aspirin for whatever was wrong, and then that would fix it. This time, it didn't work.

By noon on that Wednesday, I had taken nine aspirin and was still not feeling well. Being April third in my tax office, we were extremely busy. I had appointments with clients set up all day long and had already met with four of them that morning. It was lunchtime, so I decided to try eating, but by the time I got to the kitchen area, I knew I needed to lie down. I headed back for the front of the office where there was a couch and started collapsing before I got that far.

By God's design, my daughter was in the office that morning and was already aware my heart was the problem and that I was in denial. I was so focused on tax work there was no time to be sick. "Two weeks from now, Lord, not now, I can't be sick now. It is the beginning of April!" My manipulative pleading hadn't changed a thing.

Angela, my daughter, knew it was serious and not to hesitate to call 911. The ambulance arrived in just a few minutes, and the EMTs (emergency medical technicians) only asked a couple questions until they had made a diagnosis. I was having a heart attack. Then they moved quickly, getting me loaded into the ambulance, and we took a very fast trip to the hospital emergency room.

From the time I got to the hospital emergency, was taken to the CAF Lab, had a stent placed to open the blocked artery, and was taken upstairs to recovery, only thirty minutes had elapsed. I stayed conscious for the most part with moments of fading in and out. I do remember them literally running down a hallway and cutting my clothes to get them off. The ambulance and hospital personnel were working very fast and efficiently to save my life that day.

Had Angela not been there, I probably would not have survived, since my adult assistant repeatedly questioned if I was actually sick enough to call 911. After all, I had been working all morning without complaining.

Had the ambulance EMTs not been able to assess I had a one hundred percent blockage and was in an active heart attack, they would not have driven so very fast to the hospital, and my chances of survival would have diminished greatly.

Had the hospital personnel not run down the hallways with me on the gurney, cut my clothing off, and gotten the stent placed as fast as they did, I would not have survived. God was in control.

After coming into the hospital on Wednesday, I was scheduled to be released on the following Saturday. That Friday morning, the day before I was to be released, I had gotten up, did my walk as the nurse's had instructed, and was settled into my chair. I was looking forward to and awaiting breakfast when the nurse said for me to get back into bed.

The nurse knew before I did that I was about to have a very bad day. My blood pressure had started dropping, and they couldn't get it to stop. At noon, the doctor took me back through the CAF Lab to see if the stent had moved; it hadn't. It wasn't until early evening after they had put a pick line in with medicine going directly into my heart that things started getting better. My blood pressure had gotten down to something like 30/40 that day before the situation started turning around. I never did get my breakfast—or any other meal that day.

I was not concerned through it all. In the morning on that Friday, when I realized my strength was seeping away, I told the Lord, "I think I am going to need your help." It doesn't take a lot of words when you talk to the Lord from your heart. He is real, He is right there with you all the time, and He is listening. His peace never left me.

I was released from the hospital the following Monday. Since then, I have had numerous additional ambulance rides to the hospital emergency room over heart issues. The Lord has always been there and has always seen me through. I don't fear it because I know God has it under control.

> *Make sure that your character is free from the love of money, being content with what you have; for He himself has said,* **"I will never desert you, nor will I ever forsake you,"** *so that we confidently say,* **"The Lord is my Helper, I will not be afraid.** *What will man do to me?" (Hebrews 13:5–6, NASB 1995; emphasis mine)*

> *Beloved, I wish above all things that thou mayest prosper and* **be in health,** *even as thy soul prospereth. (3 John 1:2 KJV; emphasis mine)*

If we only serve God half-heartedly, when danger surrounds us, instead of being filled with faith, we'll find ourselves paralyzed with fear.

E.   With My Life

There was a situation in 1971 when my husband (the violent criminal one) became extremely angry with me because I would not agree to adopt a deformed, mentally retarded child he had fathered with some girl that lived in town. I had offered to move out and let him move her in. But that wasn't an option in his mind. He was very much into controlling me and he saw my adopting this child as an end to that means.

As we argued, I was standing in front of a glass sliding door when his fury took over. He picked up a gun (he kept two loaded and ready on the coffee table), grabbed me, and held the gun to my temple. I could see the trigger being pulled back past the point of firing.

I looked out the glass door at the sky and internally said, "Ready or not, here I come."

In that moment, he asked me what I was doing, and without thinking, this word came out of my mouth, "Praying."

That one word diffused the situation. He very gradually let off the trigger and was noticeably shaken for weeks over what he had almost done. He never mentioned that child again.

The part that fascinated me is that I knew the gun he picked up. I had fired it myself in the past. It had a hair trigger that went off with the slightest pressure. And yet, when it was against my head, it did not go off.

This situation happened seven years before I had the second encounter with God and committed my life to Him. I had the first encounter at four years old and knew God existed. But at this point in my life, I didn't know anything about God. Or that He could stop guns from firing. Or that He could possibly ever care about me. My self-worth was nonexistent.

God was in control. It wasn't my time to go home, and because I belonged to God, He prevented the devil's plan from working and saved my life. God knew my future, and that the day would come when my life would totally change.

> *For I know the plans that I have for you, declares the Lord, plans for prosperity and not for disaster to give you a future and a hope. (Jeremiah 29:11 NASB)*

How God Will Use Anyone

God's Will Be Done

A. Life in Hell

After my son was born in 1965, I found myself in a difficult position. My husband was in the military, collecting the family allotment funds and totally unconcerned about his pregnant wife. I moved back home with my parents a few weeks before the baby was born. And now I was faced with working, paying rent, raising a child financially on my own, a sick father that required regular daily care, and a mother that was totally taken with being a "mother" to my son. I obviously didn't know anything about babies, since I didn't have any younger siblings. And so she left all the housework, dirty cloth diapers, dishes, and bottles for me to clean each evening after work.

I had somewhat of a Cinderella complex, since my only time to even hold my son was a few minutes before bedtime while I fed him the last bottle of the day. My mother worked a midnight shift and watched over my son and father while I worked during the day. When I got home, she went to bed, and I took over doing all the cleanup from that day and preparation for the next day.

Even though disposable diapers had been invented by this time, because of the cost, we used cloth diapers. The cloth diapers had to be washed out by hand each day before being taken to the laundromat to be laundered. The milk formula we used had to be prepared each day and put into freshly washed and sterilized bottles. As a result, my work on a normal day started at 6:00 a.m. and ended at 9:00 p.m.

A Knight in Shining Armor, or so he appeared, showed up to help me. I was able to start having the government family allotment funds sent to me. He helped find an apartment for my son and myself and encouraged me to get a divorce.

In March 1968, I married the Knight in Shining Armor. It didn't take long to realize I had gotten into something bad that I couldn't get out of. I was in way over my head. Over time, he showed himself to be a violent criminal, very controlling, and very abusive in every way. In his eyes, he owned me and could do as he pleased while my son and I were to do only as he said, without question, or else.

He kept my son and me living at a poverty level of just barely enough food and a cheap roof of some type over our heads. No money, no car, no friends, no family, no freedom, though he had it all. He would disappear for days at a time and suddenly reappear at unsuspecting hours. He would come into the house in the middle of the night and demand we had to get up, get dressed, and travel to another state *now*! My young son would be allowed to sleep in the back seat, but I always had to stay sitting up and awake in the front seat of the car. He wanted the appearance of a young family to always be readily seen.

I managed to get us totally away from him one time. I was half-way across the country. His response was to go after my mother with a gun and an ultimatum. My mother didn't tell him where I was, but she did contact me and tell me I needed to call him.

That was enough to let me know he had done something serious to my mother. When I talked to him, because of his history and his "friends," I knew if I didn't go back, he would carry out his threats. My family would start having accidents and disappearing one at a time. He had the connections to have a solid alibi and appear to be totally innocent in the eyes of the law. In Detroit, at that time in history, that behavior was not unusual.

This marriage went on for ten years. Then one summer, the devil's grip started loosening. By this time, he was leaving for months at a time and not just days. He was confident he had us under control.

I believe someone somewhere had started praying because of the process of events that started happening that summer to give me a glimmer of hope. That glimmer grew and grew, and a year later, with God's help, I was able to get free from him physically and legally.

Though I never saw him again, getting free emotionally took a lot longer. I had been terrorized for ten years and suffered for a number of years with what people now call PTSD. Even thirty years later when I learned of his death, it was like a heavy load was taken off my shoulders. My son and I both breathed a sigh of relief. That threat had hung in the background over us for all those years, and we didn't realize it.

Sometimes we think that to belong to the Lord means our lives should be all happy and wonderful all the time and nothing bad should ever happen. I don't believe that is so. Sometimes we need to learn from our sufferings, as it says in the Bible that Jesus did.

> *Although He was a Son, He learned obedience from the things which **He suffered**. (Hebrews 5:8 NASB; emphasis mine)*

I needed to learn humility, among many other things, so I could later recognize and empathize with others and be obedient to do God's will. What really matters in this life is what we do for the Lord. If we never learn to look to Him as the ultimate power that He is, our commitment to do things His way may not be as strong as it needs to be. I am a strong-willed person, and it took a lot to convince me God's way is the **only** way that works and His way doesn't stop working.

God intervened for me many times over the years before I committed my life to Him. I believe I actually belonged to God since I was four years old and had that first *encounter* with Him. He was always watching over me even though I didn't show Him any faith, trust, or obedience.

> *He sent from on high, He took me; He drew me out of many waters. He delivered me from my strong enemy, from those who hated me, for they were too strong for me. They confronted me in the day of my calamity, but the LORD was my support. He also brought me forth into a broad place; He rescued me, because He delighted in me. (2 Samuel 22:17–20 NASB 1995)*

B.   Attempted Suicide

At the beginning of 1972, my husband was injured on the job when a spring wire cable broke loose, hit him in the face, and blinded him in the left eye. The hospital had him on morphine for the pain. But he was so uncontrollable in inappropriate behavior with the nurses that they released him and sent him home. This was the violent husband I nicknamed the Knight in Shining Armor.

When he was released from the hospital, the doctor gave him the strongest prescription drugs they could for the pain and for him to sleep. However, they weren't as strong as the morphine he was on in the hospital, and he was eating them like candy. He was physically forcing the local country pharmacist to keep refilling the prescriptions every couple days instead of following the monthly instructions.

The only way I could reasonably describe his behavior during that time was as a raving maniac. I even called the doctor one day and begged him to put my husband back in the hospital. They could at least put him unconscious. The doctor refused. There were a number of bad incidents over those months of recuperation.

By Easter, he was doing better and had started driving and going places again. That weekend, we traveled on one of his middle-of-the-night rush trips to Detroit and then back to central Indiana where we were living at the time. On the way back, he kept me awake all night, hollering and complaining as he drove at very high speeds. Maybe being angry helped him stay awake. I was physically exhausted, hadn't eaten for a couple of days, wanted out of this situation, but I had been unable to find any way to get free from him.

Once home, I hit my limit. The Knight left the house, and the only thing going through my mind was, *no more*. I walked to the bedroom and saw a full bottle of his prescription sleeping pills sitting on the dresser. *No more, no more*, the devil kept whispering. I swallowed the whole bottle of pills and lay down on the bed to die.

Suddenly, something inside me hollered out, *God, help me!* Then from my mind, I said, *Not even God can help me.*

But God did. In that moment, the Knight was standing in line at the local grocery store waiting to pay for a pack of cigarettes when he suddenly knew he had to go. Totally out of his "cool" character image, he threw down his money and took off running, not knowing why he felt such urgency. He came back to the house and found me. He got me to the car and raced to the closest doctor.

He walked in on the doctor while he was with a patient and physically dragged the doctor out to the car. The doctor told him I was already too far gone and he would never make it to the hospital in time. That didn't stop him. The Knight raced to the hospital seven miles away, going through parking lots to get around traffic and through red traffic lights.

The hospital emergency staff worked diligently but didn't know if I would survive. They put me in ICU on a ventilator and said it depended on how strong my heart was. Three days later, I started regaining consciousness.

My first thoughts when I realized I wasn't dead brought indescribable emotional pain that started in my feet and came all the way up. Because what I was realizing is that someday I would have to get up and go back into that hellhole of an existence again. I couldn't even die to get out of it.

I did suffer some brain damage as a result of this situation. Some of the damage I was able to overcome in a few months, but the stutter took years to overcome. And the lightning-fast response with which I could verbally respond to someone never returned.

God is faithful to those that belong to Him. He knew that relationship would eventually come to an end and that I had a bright future ahead even though I couldn't see it then. He used the very person that dug the black hole I was in to be the person to save me from death. God can use anyone or anything for His purposes to accomplish His will.

> *When the donkey saw the angel of the Lord*
> *standing in the way with his drawn sword in his*
> *hand, the donkey turned off from the way...*
> *When the donkey saw the angel of the Lord,*
> *she pressed herself to the wall...*

> *When the donkey saw the angel of the Lord, she lay down under Balaam; so Balaam was angry and struck the donkey with his stick and the Lord opened the mouth of the donkey, and she said to Balaam, "What have I done to you, that you have struck me these three times?"*
>
> *Then the Lord opened the eyes of Balaam, and he saw the angel of the Lord standing in the way with his drawn sword in his hand... (Numbers 22:23, 25, 27–28, 31 NASB 1995)*

God can even use a donkey!

> *So miserable you thought you'd be better off dead. Then you called out to God in your desperate condition; he got you out in the nick of time. He spoke the word that healed you, that pulled you back from the brink of death. So thank God for his marvelous love, for his miracle mercy to the children he loves. Offer thanksgiving sacrifices, tell the world what he's done—sing it out! (Psalm 107:18–22 MSG)*

C. Elizabeth Was Blessed

In the early 1990s, a friend at church, Elizabeth, had asked for prayer one Sunday morning. It was the practice of that church for members of the congregation to stand around the person, laying hands on them while praying.

I was standing behind Elizabeth with my right hand lightly touching her shoulder when my hand started shaking. It was bouncing on her shoulder like a nervous twitch. When I reached out with my other hand to try and stop it, I heard God ask, "Do you want me to work through you?" Hearing the Lord startled me, but I quickly said, "Yes!" and let go of my erratic arm.

My hand kept bouncing on her shoulder, stronger and stronger. Then I felt something like a red-hot flow coming out of the palm of that hand. When prayer stopped and Elizabeth turned around, she was ecstatic, saying God had been talking to her about tapping her on the shoulder.

That red-hot flow of power from God stayed in my hand and arm for hours. I tried to touch others that had come forward for prayer, but they walked away when I approached or shook off my hand. I didn't know what would happen but I touched anyone with that hand that would allow it.

God can use anyone at any time. I was just one of a group of people praying for Elizabeth. It is an honor when God chooses to work through you even if it is to help just one person.

> *These signs will accompany those who have believed: in My name they will cast out demons, they will speak with new tongues; they will pick up serpents, and if they drink any deadly poison, it will not hurt them; they will lay hands on the sick, and they will recover. (Mark 16:17–18 NASB 1995)*

> *He that hath my commandments, and keepeth them, he it is that loveth me; and he that loveth me shall be loved of my Father, and I will love him, and will manifest myself to him. (John 14:21 KJV)*

God Cares about My Self-Confidence and Self-Image

Building Self-Confidence

Delight yourself in the Lord; and He will give you the desires of your heart. Commit your way to the Lord, Trust also in Him, and He will do it. (Psalm 37:4–5 NASB)

A.   CPS Certification

Have you ever looked back over time and realized someone somewhere started praying for you because of the chain of events that transpired? That happened for me. I know someone started praying at least a year ahead of time—that is, the year before my second encounter with the Lord when I committed my life to Him and He became Lord of my life.

I didn't understand it at the time, but the iron-clad grip the devil had on my life, through my husband, started to loosen ever so slightly. Up until that time, I was not allowed to do anything away from home other than work or grocery shopping. And I was on a tight time limit for both.

To my surprise, he agreed to allow me to start taking some evening classes at the local college just down the street and spend my remaining evenings in study at home. This was in preparation for a two-day, sixteen-hour exam to earn certification as a professional secretary from the National Secretary Association.

At that time, to become a Certified Professional Secretary (CPS), the requirements included, among other things, a five-part exam with each part lasting two to four hours. They allowed a person five years to pass the entire five parts of the exam. Because the exam was so extensive, some girls concentrated on one part at a time taking one test per year.

There were seven or eight girls, all active experienced secretaries, from the company I worked for that sat for the exam with me for the first time in 1978. I was the only one in that group to pass four of the five parts. No one passed them all.

It struck me as most unusual that the easiest part was the one I missed and had to go back and retake it the next year. The test was different each year, and they only offered it once a year.

I have always felt God gave me the CPS award from the National Secretary Association in 1979 after I retook that one missed part. I never felt confidence in my ability to have earned such an honor. The Florida governor that year sent me a congratulatory letter.

I believe God gave me that certification to help my self-confidence, self-worth, and self-image. He was pulling me up from a very deep, very dark hole.

The year 1978 was when I was divorced from the violent Knight in Shining Armor, had the second *encounter* with the Lord, and started coming out of the darkness. Passing four parts on the CPS certification test did wonders to help me start seeing myself as a person and not just a wasted excuse for a human being. Then starting the new job with the USPS at a much higher pay was icing on the cake and a daily reminder I had value.

> *Are not five sparrows sold for two cents? Yet not one of them is forgotten before God. Indeed, the very hairs of your head are all numbered. Do not fear; you are more valuable than many sparrows. And I say to you, everyone who confesses Me before men, the Son of Man will confess him also before the angels of God. (Luke 12:6–8 NASB 1995)*

B. Enrolled Agent License

The Lord delivered to me the EA (Enrolled Agent) license from the Internal Revenue Service on the very day my third husband got his divorce finalized, July 1, 2002. We had been married since November 1, 1985.

The previous summer, I had asked my family for permission to study for the EA exam. It was another two-day, sixteen-hour exam with four parts, each of which lasted four hours. They allowed four years to complete the entire exam. You received credit for each part as you passed it. I was focused on passing all four parts of the exam in one year.

The study materials were new each year and based on that particular year's tax laws. The study materials were not ready for release until June each year, and the exam was four months later in October.

When I received my study materials, I calculated out how many pages I had to cover each day in order to have a chance at completion by October. It was a considerable amount of time every single day, seven days a week, thus my reasoning in asking for my family's permission.

As I would need to spend the time I had studying, I would not be able to wait on the family members like normal. It was going to require some teamwork at home to keep things done.

In August, I decided to go on a Daniel Diet—that is, nothing but vegetables and water. Surprisingly, after a week or so, my memory became noticeably sharper. That was a big help with so much detail to be retained.

I sat for the exam in October but didn't receive the results from the test until the following March. I had passed all of the four exam parts in the first sitting—a rare occurrence—but that was just the first step to receiving the EA license.

There were all kinds of FBI checks, financial check, friends and relative check, personal background check, personal ethics check, etc. to go through. It could easily be another six months or more before I would hear anything about actual licensing approval. But instead, God had my EA certificate approved, signed, and dated just three months later, on July 1, 2002.

I was out of town at the time, but when I got back and read my mail, I knew God had somehow sped the process up just for me. July first was the same day the divorce court approved the dissolution of my family as I had known it for almost seventeen years.

The destruction of my family at my husband's hands was a crushing blow from the devil. But God, He was right there with His loving arms, showing me I wasn't alone and everything was going to be okay.

The EA license was originated in 1884. There are only about 46,000 EAs practicing nationwide as compared to 669,130 CPAs. Enrolled agent status is the highest credential the IRS awards. The elite group of EAs have unlimited practice rights in representing individuals and businesses before the IRS. A lot of EAs are employees of the IRS.

EAs are the only tax professionals tested by the IRS on their knowledge of tax law and regulations. EAs adhere to a code of ethics and professional conduct, are required by the IRS to take continuing professional education (CPE), and are governed by Treasury Circular 230.

In recent years, the EA exam was reduced in size and complexity to help more people pass it and become licensed.

> *Make sure that your character is free from the love of money, being content with what you have; for He Himself has said, **"I WILL NEVER DESERT YOU, NOR WILL I EVER ABANDON YOU."** (Hebrews 13:5 NASB; emphasis mine)*

> *For the word of God is living and active and sharper than any two-edged sword, and piercing as far as the division of soul and spirit, of both joints and marrow, and able to judge the thoughts and intentions of the heart. And there is no creature hidden from His sight, but all things are open and*

laid bare to the eyes of Him with whom we have to do. Therefore, since we have a great high priest who has passed through the heavens, Jesus the Son of God, let us hold fast our confession. For we do not have a high priest who cannot sympathize with our weaknesses, but One who has been tempted in all things as we are, yet without sin. Therefore let us draw near with confidence to the throne of grace, **so that we may receive mercy and find grace to help in time of need.** *(Hebrews 4:12–16 NASB 1995; emphasis mine)*

C. Self-Confidence

From the time I first met Michael in 1983, he helped build my self-confidence by always telling me, "You can do it." He was so convincing I believed he believed in me. Someone being at my side continually and believing in me and my abilities in a positive way was something I had never experienced before.

I had ideas all the time—to do something new with cooking, with home decorating, with an educational venture—but I rarely acted on them to any degree. I just never believed I could accomplish anything that had value or mattered. And I didn't recognize those times when I had actually accomplished something. So when Michael came along with his encouraging words, I started thinking maybe I can do this. It was just one little thing after another until it came to opening the tax office.

It was a childhood dream that "if I ever had a business, I would call it Jan's Tax & Accounting." There was never any question in my mind as to what kind of business I would have. No selling house slippers, dishes, or makeup for this girl. It was numbers all the way for me.

When I was in high school, I adsorbed every class that was offered in the Business Department of the school and couldn't get enough of the practice company bookkeeping records we would get to work through. These kits gave us samples of all the normal business transactions that happen in a working business to figure out and record. They definitely connected with my love of numbers.

Later, when I completed Rhema Bible Training College in May 1998 and I started praying about what the Lord wanted me to do in ministry, He clearly said, "Get an office." That wasn't what I expected to hear, having just completed ministry school, but it was more comfortable than had He told me to *preach* or go to the mission field.

I had had a home-based business for many years, but actually stepping out to find a location (away from my home office), deal with a commercial lease and rent that location, set the office up, and start being a *real* business with employees and a door anyone could walk through took a **lot** of encouragement each step of the way.

We had moved to a new home at the beginning of 1998, and I spent the next fifteen months painting the outside and decorating the inside before I was brave enough to stop the distractions and step out and do what God had told me to do.

I was comfortable doing the work from a home office where I felt in control. It was stepping out into the public eye and feeling vulnerable that was so difficult. It was December 1999 when I found the location where I would spend the next twenty-one years and fulfill the dream God had placed on my heart in a more culturally standardized way.

The first year in operation was a financial loss due to all the start-up costs. The next year, 2001, the business just broke even. The following year, 2002, my husband moved out on January sixth, and it was just God and me from then on. My husband had been a crutch that I had to learn to live without and to put my full dependence on God. It wasn't easy and it took time, but we—God and I—got it done. And I was only blessed for having gone through the process.

God is patient with us. He knows when to give us a push and when to let us work through an obstacle with or without a crutch.

> *"For I know the plans that I have for you,"*
> *declares the Lord, "plans for prosperity and not for*
> *disaster, to give you a future and a hope." (Jeremiah*
> *29:11 NASB)*

The Lord is not slow about His promise, as some count slowness, but is patient toward you, not willing for any to perish, but for all to come to repentance. (2 Peter 3:9 NASB)

D. Sermons

I attended Rhema Bible Training College from September 1996 to May 1998. At that time, it was a two-year ministry training program. For the second year, we chose which area of ministry we wanted to specialize in (children's, missions, music, etc.) and then signed up for that group. After much prayer, God had me sign up for the Pastors' Group. This group focused on not only founding a church and pastoring a congregation but on the leadership side also.

At the very beginning, we were informed that as a part of the Pastors' Group, it was a requirement to give two ten-minute sermons in front of the class of approximately three hundred students over the course of the school year.

Considering I was the person that *never* talked, would get physically ill and miss elementary school rather than stand up in front of twenty kids in the classroom, and in high school totally fumbled a National Honor Society speech to an audience of parents and walked offstage humiliated, this was no easy task.

For the first ten-minute sermon, I was one of the very last on the presentation list. That gave me time to prepare and listen to what everyone else did. For the second sermon, to be given in the spring, I was the very first one on the presentation list. But I knew it was coming and had six months to prepare a ten-minute sermon. I actually survived presentation of each of them, but there were plenty of sleepless nights, sweat, and tears during the preparation time.

The one bright light was that I was sure, beyond a doubt, God was *not* calling me to be a preacher! His angels had to work overtime for months in helping me prepare for just ten minutes of public speaking.

However, I did gain confidence through that experience that I could at least talk in front of a group of people if I ever had to. I wasn't going to volunteer, but if the situation arose where I needed to, I knew I could do it. For me, that was a very big step.

> *And Jesus came up and spoke to them, saying, "All authority in heaven and on earth has been given to Me. Go, therefore, and make disciples of all the nations, baptizing them in the name of the Father and the Son and the Holy Spirit, teaching them to follow all that I commanded you; **and behold, I am with you always, to the end of the age.**" (Matthew 28:18–20 NASB; emphasis mine)*

> *I can do **all things** through Him who strengthens me. (Philippians 4:13 NASB; emphasis mine)*

How I Learned God Loves Me

God Loves Me!

A.   Blessings Galore

For Christmas 1990, my husband gave me a gift of two expensive pantsuit outfits and satin pajamas. They were clothing you would only expect to see very wealthy people wearing or in the movies. A couple of months earlier, I had paid off the car I was driving—a 1989 Cadillac, pearl white, fully loaded, yummy dream car. We had purchased it as a used car with eight thousand miles on it at the beginning of 1990.

So to summarize, I was living in a new house (3,200 square feet) we had just built and moved into in January 1990. We bought the Cadillac February 1990 and paid it off in November 1990, and now my husband had given me beautiful expensive clothes for Christmas. This was all part of the overall picture God was planning to show me.

There was a Christian women's conference scheduled for January 1991 in Destin, Florida. I really wanted to attend and had made a reservation at the host hotel months earlier in the summer.

When the word got around our church about the women's conference, the church leadership decided to do a group outing for all the ladies that wanted to attend. The rooms were set up at the host hotel to be four people to a room during the conference. All the potential roommates I had lined up decided to go with the church group. They were housed in an overflow hotel a few miles away.

So I drove alone in my Cadillac to the host hotel. It was a Hilton Hotel that hosted the event, and I was given a room on the thirteenth floor, looking out over the blue water of the Gulf of Mexico. Seagulls were flying outside my balcony over the sandy beach below. It was a picture-book setting.

When I first arrived, the temperature in the room was cool, so I turned the heat up before going downstairs for the welcome get-together. Upon arriving back to my room and opening the door, it was cloudy inside. At that moment, I wondered if it was fog from outside or because I had turned the heat up.

It wasn't until months later I realized it was the presence of God in that room. After entering the room, I became aware of how everything was so beautiful around me, and it was so peaceful in my room I just wanted to bask in it. I almost resented when it was time to go downstairs to another conference meeting. There was just something so wonderful and comforting about that room I didn't want to leave it. The cloud never left the room for the entire conference.

During the two-day meeting, it was a desire in my heart to say thank you to Gloria Copeland, the guest speaker. I didn't believe actually being able to speak to her was anything that could ever happen.

Then as I headed downstairs for one of the meetings, I stepped out of the elevator at the same moment she stepped out of another elevator. She looked directly at me and waited. Somehow I could tell she sensed I wanted to speak to her. I was so "in the clouds" I couldn't make words come out and only grinned from ear to ear at her. Hopefully she understood how very thankful I was for her strong example of a life walking with the Lord in spite of my foolish stance.

At one point, in my room, I felt in my heart the Lord saying, "This is what I want for you."

I understood He meant all the beauty, nice things, top-of-the-line accommodations and transportation. He didn't want me living like I was poor, broke, always going without, and pinching pennies out of fear I would run out. That was a mental state of mind I needed to change.

The love He was expressing to me is beyond my ability to put into words. There was never anything in my life that I could compare to the love God was communicating in that setting. I don't remember what the conference was about, but I'll never forget the comfort, peace, and love I felt in that room.

Food didn't even matter. After two days, I realized I hadn't eaten. I wasn't hungry, and it didn't matter in light of the peaceful comfort of being with the Spirit of God.

I left that hotel with an assurance and inner confidence of God's love for me. I had never questioned His love for other people. But even after being a committed Christian for twelve years, I had never been able to accept God could love me—until that weekend.

There was also joy. On the drive home, I was looking for a rest area to stop and rearrange my supplies. I drove and drove and drove thinking I had to be close to a rest area. Finally, I gave up and just pulled off the highway onto the shoulder. Once I pulled back onto the road, I hadn't driven more than half a mile and saw the sign for the rest area. I sensed the Lord getting a chuckle out of my impatience, and I also laughed.

There is no limit to the lengths God will go to reach His children. I had so much old baggage of rejection, abandonment, and just not being valued or cared for that it took God setting up this whole elaborate scenario and spending two days with me in that cloud to get through to me that He really does care for ME!

> *The Lord appeared to him long ago saying, "I have loved you with an everlasting love; therefore I have drawn you out with kindness. I will build you again and you will be rebuilt..." (Jeremiah 31:3–4 NASB)*

RELATIONSHIPS

Relationships

A.   God Had a Perfect Mate

If we could only realize right at the beginning God loves us so much He has everything perfectly planned out for us. Trusting Him and doing things His way is the answer to everything.

Unfortunately, when it comes to relationships, I was a very slow learner. There was so much negative I needed to unlearn that when I was looking for a new mate, my guideline was only that he not be like the past bad relationships.

It never crossed my mind to actually look for specific good traits, attitudes, or behaviors. I saw myself as so unattractive and unlovable I was overjoyed when any male looked my direction and showed any interest at all. My guideline should have been to look for what God sees as good.

It was the spring of 1986 when a pleasant-looking gentleman came to my door, inquiring about a previous owner of my home. I had lived in that home for seven years at the time and didn't know the people he was looking for. As he walked away, God said, "That is the one I would have picked."

I froze with shock! The realization that God had a *pick*, a perfect mate for me, and that I had majorly missed it by marrying someone else just a few months earlier all hit me at once.

What do I do now? God didn't answer. I considered annulling the marriage, but on what grounds? What would I say? And God wasn't saying that was the correct course of action to take, anyway.

God wasn't saying anything. I had taken marriage vows. So I did nothing.

Seventeen years later, after that marriage fell apart, I never started dating again because that memory was always in the back of my mind. It isn't okay to pick your own mate if you want God's best. God has the perfect mate and the perfect answer to any question. We just need to wait on Him to work it all out.

In hindsight, there had been warning signs upon warning signs from the beginning of the relationship that I was on a wrong road with the man I married. But my low self-esteem shoved them aside, fearing there would never be anyone else when, if I had only waited a few more months, life could have turned out a whole lot different.

When we are twenty years old and looking ahead at life, the thought of waiting until you are forty to marry seems an impossible lifetime away. You think you would be beyond your prime, beyond childbearing age. But when you are seventy and looking back at all the mistakes, wasted time, destroyed dreams, and heartache because you weren't willing to wait, then waiting until forty to marry seems like such an easier and better route to have taken.

At twenty looking forward, forty seemed too old to have children. But at seventy looking back and having had a child at twenty and another one at forty-two, the perspective is totally different. I was so much better of a parent in my forties. At forty-two, I had time to grow up myself before trying to raise a child. Unfortunately, we only get one chance at this life. I encourage you to slow down, make God the center of your decisions, and hopefully avoid the mistakes I made.

God doesn't change His mind. We don't get a rewind on time. His word is *yes* and *amen.*

> *For all the promises of God in him are yea, and in him Amen, unto the glory of God by us. (2 Corinthians 1:20 KJV)*

How I Learned God Provides

God the Provider

A. Situation #1—Job Change

In June 1978, my twelve-year-old son, John, and I were living in a duplex that happened to be next door to my mom's house in Bradenton, Florida. I worked as a secretary in the corporate offices at the local Tropicana manufacturing plant. I was being paid an hourly rate just over minimum wage.

Our financial budget was such that we ate the same basic foods every week, restricted driving to the same round-trip mileage to work and one grocery stop each week, lived with bare necessities and nothing extra. We didn't have a telephone or use the heat or air-conditioning in order to keep the expenses at a minimum and within our income.

When I came to the Lord that year, I had just received an $8 per week raise in pay. A tithe on my gross would have been $10 per week. Logic told me if I were to tithe, I would come up short on the very limited budget we were already following. I didn't have any *extra* at all.

My friend and mentor, Vivian, who had led me to the Lord, said tithing was something God said to do in the Bible. Even though I didn't understand why or know how I would pay the bills, I decided to start tithing—on the gross. Somehow that next month, I was able to pay all the bills even though I didn't understand logically how it happened. Logically, I should have been short on funds by the end of the month, but we weren't.

In the early spring of that year, I had taken the employment test for the US post office. Then in August, I got a call that I was being hired as a mail carrier. My hourly pay doubled, and they even paid me extra for travel time, training, and even more I never figured out what for. They just kept giving me checks.

I allowed a little extra in our budget to make life more comfortable but started saving the rest. I didn't trust all this extra income would last and was afraid they had overpaid me for the checks I didn't understand. I expected them to ask to have it back.

I was so, so thankful to have that job no matter how hard the work was. I was thirty-three years old, and financially we had finally gotten to a point where I had more than barely enough for survival. And there was even some left over to help us get ahead.

There were so many things God did for us during that time. One was that someone at work talked me into taking the USPS test to begin with. Then I actually qualified for the job. At that time, military people were given preferential treatment and given a five-point bonus on the test. That meant nonmilitary people had to do even better to get a high-enough score to be selected. There were hundreds of applicants, mostly ex-military. It was God's grace that I came in second from the top and was hired.

Then once on the job, I quickly found out women were thought to be too frail to be a mail carrier and had to deal with the discrimination and prove myself. I was the second woman to invade that particular male-dominated mail carrier group. The first woman was a widow of a previous mail carrier and was given grace because of her husband.

God's grace was with me all the way. Our road to prosperity wasn't without difficulties, but at least we were on the road now. God has a way of always making things work out.

And He directed the people to recline on the
ground; and taking the seven loaves, He gave thanks
and broke them, and started giving them to His

disciples to serve, and they served them to the peo-
ple. They also had a few small fish; and after He
had blessed them, He told the disciples to serve these
as well. And they ate and were satisfied; and they
picked up seven large baskets full of what was left
over of the broken pieces. About four thousand men
were there; and He dismissed them. (Mark 8:6–9
NASB)

B.   Situation #2—Buying First House

The next year, after I had committed my life to the Lord and had started working at the USPS, my friend/mentor Vivian and her husband had moved from Florida back to New Jersey. They were only in Florida for six months after I came to the Lord.

Then one day, Vivian called and told me they were trying to sign a real estate contract to sell their Florida home, and she felt very strongly she needed to talk to me first. We talked for a while before the first flicker, which then became a thought, and that thought turned into an idea that it might be possible and that somehow I might actually be able to purchase their house.

I had been in the market and looking for a smaller, less-expensive home. I was discouraged and had given up on finding anything because I couldn't cover the down payment the banks required on a normal real estate contract. I had been saving, but it just wasn't enough yet. What Vivian was suggesting was an entirely different kind of a deal buying directly from them.

As it worked out, eliminating the realtor and normal extensive closing costs, I was able to assume their mortgage at the bank with no money outlay for the mortgage transfer or closing. Then I got a loan from my mom combined with the savings I had accumulated so I could pay Vivian and her husband their equity in the house and bring the total up to the selling price they needed. God worked it all out for us, so we both won and walked away with a good deal. They had the funds they needed, and I had a home of our own for my son and myself.

An added bonus for me was that the home was very hard to find. It was buried in the middle of a subdivision on a street that was only one block long. This was long before GPS was ever thought of. It took more than a few tries to find your way to that house without making wrong-turns. That helped me feel more secure and especially helped protect us during the following months when the very angry, tarnished Knight in Shining Armor was trying to find me.

> *And God is able to make all grace overflow to you, so that, always having all sufficiency in every-thing, you may have an abundance for every good deed. (2 Corinthians 9:8 NASB)*

C. Situation #3—JTA Billing System

During January 1991, the Lord started talking to me about allowing clients to decide on their fees for my services through Jan's Tax and Accounting Service (JTA). For six months, I tried to explain to the Lord how that would not work. You cannot run a business letting people decide what they want to pay you. It isn't practical. It isn't sensible. I went to school. They will take total advantage of me. It will never work, and on and on I went.

By the time it was summer, God hadn't answered a word, and I had worn myself out with all the logical ways it wouldn't work. So one day, sitting in my office, my forefinger pointing to heaven, I said, "Okay, I will do it your way. But if I need money, I am coming to you!!"

When the next tax season started and I explained to clients how I was allowing them to decide on their fee for my services because God had shown me seven blessings in 2 Corinthians 9:6–11 for a cheerful giver, it met with dumb stares. People were shocked. They weren't sure whether they should take me seriously or possibly take off running. But for the most part, they paid me the same they had paid the year prior.

That is, except for one client. He had created a mess with his taxes, didn't keep receipts, and I spent hours talking with him, trying to find something that would help his situation. When we finally finished his return and I told him about my new billing system of allowing him to decide what to pay, he just chuckled and threw a $10 bill on my desk, saying, "Ha, sure, I'll tip you," and sat down in his chair.

I accepted his insult without saying a word and continued organizing papers on my desk. When I looked up at him again, the Lord let me see his countenance dropping like something pouring over his head and running down. When that man came back the next year, he had a totally different attitude and paid me a reasonable rate.

Through that one man, God let me see He really was in charge and that He was watching over me. From then on, I never concerned myself with the dollar amount I received from any individual client. For the next twenty-nine years, I continued to allow clients to set their own rates for individual tax preparation. And I prayed that each one would receive the seven blessings of a cheerful giver.

Every year there were people taking advantage and playing the financial games with their tax preparation fee, but there were also people that blessed me over and above any reasonable rate. And I never came up short. The money was always there to pay the bills no matter how lean the devil would make situations look.

Over time I saw people go through a process of disbelief, then the desire for self-interest and taking advantage, then the realization that something real was here, and a softening of their heart. Some people had to test me longer than others, but eventually I would see that softening, that understanding show up. I am sure God spoke different things to different people, but it was always Him communicating with them as individuals to show them how much He really cared for them.

*Now I say this: the one who sows sparingly will also reap sparingly, and the one who sows generously will also reap generously. Each one must do just as he has decided in his heart, not reluctantly or under compulsion, for God loves a cheerful giver. And God is able to make **all grace overflow to you**, so that, always **having all sufficiency** in everything, you* *may have **an abundance for every good deed**; as it is written:*

> *"HE SCATTERED ABROAD,*
>
> *HE GAVE TO THE POOR,*
>
> *HIS RIGHTEOUSNESS ENDURES FOREVER."*

*Now He who supplies seed to the sower and bread for food will supply and **multiply your seed for sowing** and increase the **harvest of your righteousness;** you will be **enriched in everything** for all liberality, **which through us is producing thanksgiving** to God. (2 Corinthians 9:6–11 NASB; emphasis mine)*

Seven Blessings of a Cheerful Giver

1. Grace (God's favor)
2. All sufficiency in everything
3. An abundance for good works
4. Plenty of seed to sow
5. Righteousness (right standing with God)
6. To be enriched in everything
7. To cause others to thank God

D. Situation #4—Receiving Funds for School

During tax season in 1996, a man called for a tax appointment that had been referred by a friend he was working with in North Carolina and who knew me from when I lived in Florida and that I was now living in Oklahoma. This gentleman and his wife were traveling from where he had been working in North Carolina back to their home in Enid, Oklahoma.

They stopped in Tulsa to see me on their trip home, and when we had completed his tax returns, to my amazement, he paid me $1,000 for the tax preparation. This was no ordinary situation. I knew this payment was for something special when the gentleman told me the Lord had directed him to pay me that amount.

A couple of months later, that $1,000 was going to be exactly what I needed. That spring, my husband had been attending Oral Roberts University, and I expected him to continue again in the fall for the following school year. However, in July, he changed his mind and signed up to attend Rhema Bible Training College.

I was *not* about to let him go to Bible School and leave me sitting at home! Attending Rhema Bible Training College had been a dream of mine since I had first heard about the school. I had continually set my dreams aside for the desires of my family. But not this time!

So with the funds from that special gentleman during tax season, I was able to pay my tuition to attend Rhema Bible Training College right along with my husband. Classes were daily from 8:00 a.m. to noon or 1:00 p.m., which allowed time to transport our daughter, Angela, back and forth from school and for my husband to work a midnight shift. We had a busy schedule, but we were both able to attend school and keep things going with the family.

The Holy Spirit was talking every day in those classrooms and hallways. It was glorious! After two years of study, we graduated, and I was sorry to see it end. It was such a sea of blessing and revelation knowledge, and it all started with that gentleman traveling from North Carolina.

That man had told me his story during our time together. He was a heavy equipment operator that had a bulldozer flip over on top of him. He was buried and severely injured but still alive. He managed to tell the Lord if he could get him out of this mess, he would follow Him and do whatever He wanted. He had not been living for the Lord prior to this accident. Through a number of miracles, he was rescued and eventually released from the hospital to go home to Enid, Oklahoma.

I was able to stay in contact with this client for a couple of years, and then he went home to be with the Lord. God brings about some amazing situations to fulfill His purposes.

Give thanks to the LORD, call upon His name;
Make His deeds known among the peoples. Sing to

Him, sing praises to Him; Tell of all His wonders.
Boast in His holy name; May the heart of those who
seek the LORD *be joyful. (Psalm 105: 1–3 NASB)*

E.   Situation #5—Living on Bare Essentials

When my husband moved out on January 6, 2002, suddenly I found myself going from a middle-class income and lifestyle to a situation with no income other than the $750/month from a rental house we owned. The bills and responsibilities hadn't changed, only the income. I was looking poverty in the face again, as I had so many years earlier when my now adult son had been a child. This time, I had a fourteen-year-old daughter to support (without the help of child support again).

It was the beginning of a new year and new tax season. My business was getting established and had just closed out the previous year at a breakeven point financially. My time from 8:00 a.m. to 8:00 p.m. daily was required in the office to keep the business open and operational. This eliminated the option of getting a second job to earn personal income. And I couldn't take money out of the business, since it was just generating enough income to pay its own bills.

I might have qualified for a loan, but that has never been my way of doing things. If I can't pay for what I need, then how would I ever be able to pay someone else back for a loan? Being honorable to pay what I owe has always been of high importance to me. I am not against borrowing and have used loans but only when I have a solid plan for repayment.

On paper, my daughter and I could survive on $750 a month as long as the tenants paid their rent on time and there weren't any extra expenses. The $750 would cover my tithe, food, basic utilities, and gas for the car. I turned off the television, internet, and security system and did yard services myself. But there were still extras like insurance, taxes, school supplies, extra fees for her private Christian school and the athletic programs she took part in.

Week by week, we kept surviving. Somehow checks showed up in the mail for "surveys" I had taken that I didn't remember. We got food from a ministry program and would find things on sale, or people would give us things we needed when they didn't know we needed them. I did not share our financial situation with anyone.

Our budget was tight, and I cried for a year not knowing how it was going to work out on the long term, but God stayed faithful to us. We always had what we needed for the moment, and I always kept tithing. The tenants always paid their rent on time and even did any repairs on that property without passing the cost on to me. By the end of 2002, my business income had doubled, and it continued to double again the following year. My business income never stopped growing each year until I retired January 1, 2021.

> *And my God will supply all your needs according to His riches in glory in Christ Jesus. (Philippians 4:19 NASB)*

F. Situation #6—Expanding Office Space

Unexpectedly at the beginning of January 2009, the unit in the shopping center next door to my business became vacant. They seemingly moved out overnight.

The unit my tax office was in was overcrowded, and we seriously needed more space. It was the beginning of tax season, and I was already busy with client work. So I just roughed out on paper what I could afford, how I planned to use the unit, and presented it to the landlord.

To my surprise, the landlord accepted my offer! The offer was approximately what I had paid when I first rented there ten years earlier. I didn't know at the time, but that vacant unit was actually larger than the one I was in by two hundred square feet. Also, there was another offer on the table from a chiropractor, and the unit had already been set up for that type of business from the chiropractor that had just moved out.

It was the hand of God to have that landlord accept a business deal that was based on a ten-year-old rental rate for less square footage. Considering this unit was 20 percent larger, he was receiving an even lower rate figured on a square-footage basis. Plus, he gave up having the new tenant at current rental rates when the unit was already set up for that type of business. It would have required only minimal, if any, build-out for the new tenant.

An added bonus that I hadn't even considered was the build-out to make the unit workable for us. The landlord handled all the build-out, which totaled $6,300, and didn't mention a word about me reimbursing the cost. The build-out should have been my responsibility. Normally the tenant pays for any changes that are required to the unit to accommodate their business, not the landlord. I didn't have $6,300 at the time, and had I known, the whole deal would have fallen through. God worked all the details out while my mind and attention were stuck on taxes.

The Christian Library was established in 2002, and I had been housing it around the walls of the tax office. By 2009, overstuffed bookcases covered all the wall space, and we could barely function as a tax office. God came to the rescue when that unit next door became vacant. We moved the tax office to the new space, which had a reception counter and separate office rooms, and allowed the original unit to become a full-fledged library with rows of bookcases.

The Christian Library continually grew for an additional seven years. God provided books through donations, gave me the ideas on how to arrange the shelving and set up the tracking systems and cataloging for the books. It was a free library, like the public libraries, and we just housed nothing but Christian books.

Moving day in 2009 was another God orchestrated event. It was the beginning of February when the build-out construction was completed. By this time, the tax office was very busy. We closed for one day and were able to move everything.

That included getting the phone, fax, and internet moved by the phone company. In addition, we were so crowded the furniture had to be moved in a specific order to allow room to get past the things that were staying in that old unit.

Tearing desks down, moving and setting them back up, moving full file cabinets, hanging cupboards on the wall, and getting everything set back up, organized, and ready to work was a major project.

Through the physical labor of a half dozen of His children, somehow God managed to get it all done, and we were back open for business the next day.

> *Delight yourself in the Lord; And He will give you the desires of your heart. Commit your way to the Lord, trust also in Him, and He will do it. (Psalm 37:4–5 NASB)*

G.   Situation #7—Christian Library Dream

The Christian Library idea had started when I first became a committed Christian and found out the public libraries didn't carry all the books that were being referred to me to read. I had to buy to read them. My thought was, *Wouldn't it be nice if there were a library where I could check these books out instead of buying them.*

I started collecting Christian books wherever I could find them. In 2000, I set up a nonprofit organization for the library and housed it around the walls of my tax office. It grew until we expanded in 2009 and I had enough space to separate the two businesses. Then the Christian Library continued to grow until I had to close it in 2016 due to health/labor reasons. God said it had had its season.

During prayer one day in 2010, so proud of how my Christian Library dream was developing, I asked God what His vision for a Christian library would be. God said His vision for a Christian library is that "they should be around the world like McDonald's hamburgers."

That concept shook me to the core. First, I ran from the thought, and then I started thinking about how I could ever possibly do such a thing to fulfill God's dream. At one point, I prayed and then started looking for additional locations, but nothing ever came of it. God heard my prayer, but He wasn't answering.

Finally, I realized it wasn't for me to expand and accomplish God's dream. I had tried. I had figured out a possible plan for expansion but could never get anywhere with it because God wasn't in it.

What He did do is put me in contact with Joseph. Joseph would take used Christian books and ship them overseas to create libraries in foreign countries. Our books became a part of libraries established in Turkey, Egypt, other Middle Eastern areas, and the reference books were sent to Kenneth Copeland Bible College in Fort Worth, Texas. We also donated books directly to a ministry to Native American Indians in New Mexico. So even though my Christian Library didn't multiply and go around the world like McDonalds', the Christian books did.

> *Trust in the LORD and do good; Live in the land and cultivate faithfulness. Delight yourself in the LORD; And He will give you the desires of your heart. Commit your way to the LORD, Trust also in Him, and He will do it.*
>
> *The steps of a man are established by the LORD, And He delights in his way. When he falls, he will not be hurled down, Because the LORD is the One who holds his hand. (Psalm 37:3–5, 23–24 NASB)*

HOW I LEARNED TO BE PROSPEROUS FINANCIALLY

Prosperity can mean a lot of different things to different people. To some, it might be having friends or a large family, having lots of material goods, or owning a yacht. And yet others it could mean just having a wood floor in their home instead of dirt. I can remember years when prosperity for me was spelled P-E-A-C-E. However, the following situations deal with finances because I have learned how very much God wants to bless and prosper His children if they will just trust Him and obey His direction.

Houses and Finances

A.   Paying Off New House in Florida

From 1988 to 1990, we were in the process of buying land and building a new home. Deciding on the location and specific land was easy compared to deciding on the house size, layout, and all the specific decisions about details that go into building a house.

Being an accountant, I figured the finances on what we could afford, and my husband, being the eccentric, found countless ways to spend it all and more. We finally agreed on a floor plan with 3,200 square feet, two and a half car garage on one acre of ground five miles east of the town of Bradenton, Florida. We moved into our new home in January 1990.

A couple of years earlier after learning about "owe no man," by God's direction, I had paid off the home we were living in. I planned to sell it and use the equity to help pay for the new home. The plan was, if we needed more funds due to building costs, to only have a small mortgage on the new home, which we could pay off within a few years.

However, that was my plan, not God's, and it didn't work. I put the house up for sale and had lots of people, including real estate sales personnel, say, "Oh, this will sell fast." But it didn't. And it didn't. And it didn't. We were down to time to move when finally the Lord said, "Rent this house and use the rental income as additional principal payment, and the new house will be paid off in five years."

Being true to my nature, I told Him, "That won't work!" However, considering our situation, I did what God had said and, after we moved, rented the house out.

For four and a half years, I kept saying and believing it will be years and years before this house mortgage is paid, and we are out of debt again. The balance due on the mortgage was dropping each month, as I applied the full rental income as additional principal payment, but it just didn't register with me until we were over four years into it.

Then one day, I suddenly realized, between the additional principal payments and the increased amount from the regular payment going toward the principal, the loan was going to be paid off within a year. Once I accepted it, it was only a few months later when we made the final payment, and that new home was totally ours. Plus, we still owned the old home as a rental property!

Additional principal payments apply directly and totally to the principal loan balance. They not only reduce the balance on the loan, but they also reduce the amount of interest that will be charged on the next month's regular payment. As a result, more of that next month's payment goes toward paying the actual loan amount off. It is somewhat of a double whammy on that loan balance each month.

I had learned the weakness of buying things on credit many years earlier after my son was born. Going back to work required getting new clothes that fit. I used my mom's store credit to buy three dresses. The dresses were almost totally worn out before I finally finished making the payments on them. I learned from that experience to not buy things on a monthly payment plan when I couldn't pay cash. It was better to go without, find used clothing, shop yard sales, or just wait rather than get caught in that trap again.

When it comes to mortgages, if you just make your regular payments for thirty years, you will have in effect paid about two to three times as much for that property by the time you pay it off. ($100,000 loan paid over thirty years will net approximately $200,000 in interest, depending on the interest rate, for a total out-of-pocket cost of $300,000). Now, by using additional principal payments, you can cut that total amount paid down drastically, as the Lord showed me. We had taken out a thirty-year mortgage on that new house. With the additional principal payments, it was paid off in five years. I intentionally got a thirty-year mortgage to get the regular monthly payment lower. Then I intentionally hit it every month with additional principal payment. That was God's system. Tithing always came first, of course.

God's system versus the world's way:

> *"Would anyone rob God? Yet you are robbing Me! But you say, 'How have we robbed You?' In tithes and offerings. You are cursed with a curse, for you are robbing Me, the entire nation of you! Bring the whole tithe into the storehouse, so that there may be food in My house, and put Me to the test now in this," says the* LORD *of armies, "if I do not open for you the windows of heaven and pour out for you a blessing until it overflows. Then I will rebuke the devourer for you, so that it will not destroy the fruit of your ground; nor will the vine in the field prove fruitless to you," says the* LORD *of armies, "All the nations will call you blessed, for you will be a delightful land," says the* LORD *of armies. (Malachi 3:8–12 NASB)*

> *Owe nothing to anyone except to love one another; for he who loves his neighbor has fulfilled the law. (Romans 13:8 NASB 1995)*

*The rich rules over the poor, And the borrower
becomes the lender's slave. (Proverbs 22:7 NASB)*

B.   Moving to Texas

In July 1994, we moved from Florida to Texas. My husband had traded mail routes within the US post office system with a fellow mail carrier that lived in Destin, Texas. We were moving there, and he was moving to Florida. We had a deadline to be in Destin for my husband to report for work.

To facilitate this move, it required selling my business, making arrangements for someone to manage our rental house and someone to live in the new home we had just built four years prior, along with running multiple yard sales, rehoming some pets, and packing what we didn't sell or give away.

I was opposed to the move until one day, when I was starting to pray against the spirit behind this idea of uprooting our family and moving halfway across the country, the Lord stopped me and told me to follow my husband. I didn't like it, but I wasn't going to oppose what I knew the Lord had said. The next question was, how? It seemed an impossible task.

God said, "Take $50,000 cash with you. Arrive on Sunday, find a house to buy on Monday, close on Wednesday, unload on Thursday, and turn the rental truck in on Friday." Then we could go to the Southwest Believers' Convention in Fort Worth, Texas, which started the following Monday morning. We had gone to that convention religiously every year since 1985. I wasn't willing to miss it.

The plan sounded simple enough except for the $50,000. Where was I going to get $50,000 cash? As it turned out, with the profit from that year's tax season, selling my business, adding our savings and yard sale profits, we had the $50,000 plus some extra for traveling and closing costs on the house we would find. We had been homeowners for a long time and didn't want to rent temporarily and then have to move a second time.

The night before we left, we had dinner at a friend's home. It was their custom to have group prayer before exiting their home.

The wife, Christine, said during prayer, "A man is going to sell you a home for less than he wants for it." As it turned out, her prophecy was accurate.

We left on Saturday and arrived at a motel in Destin, Texas, Sunday afternoon with our large rental truck and my husband's Dodge diesel pickup truck fully loaded and pulling a car carrier with my car on it, which was also fully loaded with my office equipment. We didn't have any wasted space or empty holes in our load.

We rested that Sunday afternoon and went house hunting first thing Monday morning. After looking at the first house for sale, it suddenly occurred to me we needed a *vacant* home! We didn't have thirty days to allow someone to move out. We needed to close and move in within two days.

With this in mind, the real estate salesman said there was one vacant home in this small town that he was aware of. It was owned by another real estate person. We went to look at the house, and it seemed perfect—a four-bedroom brick exterior sitting on two acres on the side of a hill with a long, curved, tree-covered driveway up to the house. It was a picture you would expect to see in a *Better Homes & Garden* magazine.

The real estate person that owned the property wanted $57,000 (remember, this was the 1990s and a small town). When I told him I had $50,000, he said, "No, no, I can't do that," and started pacing the floor.

We sat cordially visiting with our real estate salesman while the property owner paced and mumbled to himself and paced some more. He came over a couple of times with counteroffers, but I had to say, "No, I only have $50,000 cash to offer."

Finally, he said, "Okay, my final offer, $51,000, and I will pay all the closing costs." That sounded reasonable, since I had $1,000 set aside for closing costs.

We signed the papers on Wednesday and started unloading the truck first thing Thursday morning. Our rental agreement required we turn the truck in on Friday, which we did.

I spent Friday and Saturday unpacking necessities, and on Sunday, we headed for Fort Worth to attend the Southwest Believers' Convention that opened at nine on Monday morning.

What God had told me proved out completely. Numerous people were skeptical and even considered it humorous when I had shared God's plan in the beginning. But God is true to His word, and it all worked out just like He said. I never looked at God's instructions from a rational or business perspective. I just knew it was what God had said, and that settled it.

The Lord said to Joshua, "See, I have given Jericho into your hand, with its king and the valiant warriors. You shall march around the city, all the men of war circling the city once. You shall do so for six days. Also seven priests shall carry seven trumpets of rams horns before the ark; then on the seventh day you shall march around the city seven times, and the priests shall blow the trumpets. It shall be that when they make a long blast with the ram's horn, and when you hear the sound of the trumpet, all the people shall shout with a great shout and the wall of the city will fall down flat, and the people will go up every man straight ahead." (Joshua 6:2–5 NASB 1995)

Then on the seventh day, they rose early at the dawning of the day and marched around the city in the same manner seven times; only on that day they marched around the city seven times. At the seventh time, when the priests blew the trumpets, Joshua said to the people "Shout, for the Lord has given you the city."

So the people shouted, and priests blew the trumpets; and when the people heard the sound of the trumpet, the people shouted with a great shout and the wall fell down flat, so that the people went

> *up into the city, every man straight ahead, and they*
> *took the city. (Joshua 6:15–16, 20 NASB 1995)*

C.   Moving to Tulsa, Oklahoma (Part 1)

We had only been in Texas a couple of months when the Lord spoke to my husband and said we were supposed to be in Tulsa, not Texas. My husband retreated from sharing this wonderful news with me for a number of months—actually, until the following spring of 1995. Considering we had two houses in Florida and now one in Texas, and he wanted to move to Tulsa? Needless to say, I was not a happy camper.

When I quit shaking my head in total disbelief, the only sensible thing seemed to be to sell the big house in Florida. It was only five years old and a beautiful property. The only problem turned out to be that the "friends" we had living in the house didn't want to move out or put any effort into selling the home or making it available for anyone interested in looking at it. Plus, they had quit managing the rental home, so the tenants were also refusing admittance to anyone. In the meantime, my husband had made arrangements to start work in Tulsa the middle of July—the week after the Southwest Believers' Convention in Fort Worth, Texas, we always attended.

By June, I was so frustrated I wrote "For Sale" on a piece of wood, walked to the end of the driveway of the Texas house we were living in, and stuck it in the ground. By the time I had walked back up to the house, cars started coming up the driveway.

I hadn't cleaned or done anything to prepare this Texas house to sell. Plus, my in-laws were visiting, and we were getting ready to go out to dinner. That was on a Saturday afternoon. By the following Tuesday (three days later), I had a signed contract. The buyer needed an FHA mortgage that I was told later typically takes at least forty-five days. We had thirty days at that point before we had to be in Tulsa.

As it worked out, at the end of thirty days, we closed on the house in Texas in the morning on Wednesday, drove the large rental truck and the Dodge diesel pickup truck with the car carrier behind loaded with my car (same scenario we had done one year prior coming from Florida) to Tulsa, and closed that same afternoon on the home we were buying. On Thursday, we unloaded the rental truck and turned it in on Friday. We had the routine down. I unpacked essentials on Friday and Saturday, and on Sunday, we left for the Southwest Believers' Convention in Fort Worth, Texas, which was starting Monday morning at nine.

Now the home in Texas, we sold for $57,000. That was the original sales price from the gentleman we purchased it from exactly one year previously. We had paid him $50,000 because that was what God had told me to bring from Florida. The house in Tulsa that we purchased is another story. See "Moving to Tulsa, Oklahoma (Part 2)."

> *"For I know the plans that I have for you,"*
> *declares the Lord, "plans for prosperity and not for*
> *disaster, to give you a future and a hope." (Jeremiah*
> *29:11 NASB)*

D. Moving to Tulsa, Oklahoma (Part 2)

When we knew my husband's transfer had gone through and the date he would be starting work in Tulsa, Oklahoma, we made an appointment with a branch office in Tulsa of a national real estate company to look at houses to buy.

Since our time in Tulsa for house shopping was limited to one Saturday afternoon, I had chosen a well-known national company and sent specifics ahead of time on what we were looking for and the approximate area we were interested in. It was my hope, being a national company, the real estate salesman would have done some homework and have a select group of homes for us to look at that fit the guidelines I had sent.

Unfortunately, the real estate person started taking us to all kinds of houses that weren't at all what I had requested, though they acknowledged having received my letter of instructions. The last one he was going to show us was in the general location I had requested, but when he got there, we couldn't get access to view the home.

As the real estate person was turning around in the cul-de-sac, preparing to leave that neighborhood, I saw a "For Sale" sign in the yard of a home that looked very promising. Even though the sign was for their company, the real estate person didn't know about this property, and we had to park and wait while he called on the phone and found out it had just been listed that morning. We were able to view the home later that day, come to a purchase agreement, and make arrangements with the owner to do the closing in the afternoon on the same day we were to close on the Texas house in the morning.

One thing I had been told after arriving in Tulsa was that we could not qualify for a mortgage because we hadn't lived in the state for two years or owned any other property in Oklahoma. We owned property outright without mortgages in Florida and Texas but could not qualify for a mortgage this time. Financially this made no sense to me, since I could prove we had the assets. This just added another layer of frustration, since it meant we had to buy with cash again. I couldn't rely on getting a mortgage this time to take the pressure off the finances.

It was imperative to sell the house in Texas to have the rest of the funds needed to pay for the Tulsa home. Again, God worked it all out from the "that day's new real estate listing on the house we were buying" to "closing an FHA loan in thirty days when forty-five days is the minimum." It all went smoothly even with my continual state of frustration over the roadblocks and problems that kept erupting.

God was so faithful in spite of my shortcomings. For two years in a row, he had us travel to a new location, find and buy a home in a day and use cash for the purchase, and get unloaded in a day so we could attend the Southwest Believers' Convention in Fort Worth, Texas, the following Monday. That isn't coincidence, that's God!

We spent a year in Texas because we didn't get the location right the first time, but God still brought us to where He wanted us, the specific week of the year He wanted us there. Through the years, God had taught me how to buy not only cars for cash but now even houses.

Owe no man anything, except to love him.

> *Owe nothing to anyone except to love one another; for the one who loves his neighbor has fulfilled the Law. (Romans 13:8 NASB)*

> *So I said, I will bring you up out of the oppression of Egypt to the land of the Canaanite, the Hittite, the Amorite, the Perizzite, the Hivite, and the Jebusite, **to a land flowing with milk and honey.** (Exodus 3:17 NASB; emphasis mine)*

> *The sheep listen to his (the Shepherd's) voice and heed it; and he calls his own sheep by name and brings (leads) them out. (John 10:3 AMPC)*

E.   Investing and Multiplication

During 2004, when finances were tight, I received a $25,000 inheritance payment from the sale of my mother's home in Florida. I prayed a lot about what to do with those funds. We were managing financially, so rather than just allow our life to be more comfortable for the moment, I decided to invest that money. Also, I did a lot of research on various investments and what would be good at the time. There were five mutual funds that I settled on. I felt comfortable putting $5,000 into each one of them.

Within seven years, each $5,000 investment had grown to approximately $30,000. Normal broker-directed investments are expected to double in ten years ($5,000 to $10,000). Even using Dave Ramsey's Financial Peace teaching that mutual funds average 12 percent annual growth, the total would only have been $12,503 in each account after seven years. What happened was totally God's multiplication. The timing, the specific investments, only God knew the results that would come.

Since then, I have moved some of the money to other investments, and some I have kept as originally invested and watched it continue to grow. The growth hasn't been as fast as at the beginning (those first seven years), but overall the investments have averaged about 15 percent annual growth. If the return on investment started dropping in a certain fund and I felt the inner witness uncomfortableness, I would look for other investments. This was all led by God. My decisions have all been made after prayer and trusting the Holy Spirit inside to guide me.

I don't make investment decisions based on my head knowledge, though I did have a securities license for a time. I learned the fallacy of just trusting what I thought or what "experts" said when I first started investing, and losing money, some forty years ago. Now I use my head knowledge to help narrow the potential investments and then I trust the Holy Spirit to guide my decisions in the specifics. I don't rush into anything. Many times I have found an investment I thought was really good, but when I gave it time, the Holy Spirit would show me another one that was even better.

Owe no man anything but to love him—buy cars for cash, buy houses for cash, invest and watch it grow at God's rate of return, not the world's. The first steps are to learn to live on less than what you have coming in and be totally debt-free. That is accomplished by God's budget plan, which is tithe 10 percent, save 10 percent and live on the 80 percent.

Never underestimate the importance or power of tithing. That is really the first step in trusting God. If you truly trust God, then you need to follow His direction with your finances. If you want Him to lead you in an area, then you have to trust Him in that area.

You can't expect Him to get you out of a financial mess when you won't do what He says, can you?

The key to success in any area is having a personal relationship with God and doing things His way. Trust and obey. Look to God, not to people. The world will *always* be going the opposite direction, but that doesn't matter. Trust God and He will never fail you.

> *Because they hated knowledge and did not*
> *choose the fear of the Lord. They would not accept*
> *my counsel, they spurned all my reproof. So they*

shall eat of the fruit of their own way and be satiated with their own devices. For the waywardness of the naive will kill them, and the complacency of fools will destroy them.

But he who listens to me shall live securely and will be at ease from the dread of evil. *(Proverbs 1:29–33 NASB 1995; emphasis mine)*

WHEN GOD TAUGHT ME ABOUT ARROGANCE

Arrogance

A. Buying the Cadillac

It was February 1990, and we had just moved into the new house five miles east of town a couple of weeks prior. A friend from church owned a car dealership in town that was closing and clearing out all their inventory. One day, as we were driving past his dealership, we decided to stop just to look. We weren't in the market for a new car just yet, though it was in the near future.

The car we were driving was a gas guzzler, and living out of town now made it more of an issue, but I was determined we weren't going to get a loan to buy a car. I was steadfast in my determination that we needed to wait until we had the finances available.

As the salesman was leading us out to the lot, we walked past some other customers, and I made a remark intended for the salesman that "if I can't pay cash for it, I don't want it!"

I had no sooner made that statement when I realized those people had heard me. It also registered just how arrogant it probably sounded to someone else. My thought was to not go in debt by using credit, but people don't understand by my thought; they understand by the spoken words.

We were looking at a Cadillac that was one year old, fully loaded, with eight thousand miles on it. It was a real dream car, probably the nicest and most expensive car on the used car lot at the time. We ended up buying that car with a loan that at the time I expected to pay off within "ninety days same as cash."

Life happened, and it took ten very long months of making payments and realizing how wrong I had been before I could actually get out of the mess I had created with my mouth.

God let me suffer through those months so I would learn words matter.

Once spoken, you can't ever take words back. God created the whole universe with words. Our words can also have lasting effects on other people. I may never know the full extent of the damage those words could have caused.

When there is correction, there is also grace. We went on to own that car for nine years. It was the best car, beautiful pearl-white color, and so easy to handle. I could park it on a dime and maneuver it so easy. Plus, it was a prestigious type of car that gave me pride to be able to own something so nice. I totally enjoyed that car all the years we had it.

> *If you have been ensnared by the words of your mouth, or caught by the words of your mouth. (Proverbs 6:2 NASB)*

> *May the words of my mouth and the meditation of my heart be acceptable in Your sight, Lord, my rock and my Redeemer. (Psalm 19:14 NASB)*

How God Taught Me He Has Given Us Authority Over Demons

Demons

A. Demons in Bloomington House

Before I knew the Lord, we were renting a home in Bloomington, Indiana, and there were demons living in that house. Before we moved in, people had said it was haunted, but we didn't really take them seriously.

Then one night, a demon woke me from a sound sleep. It looked like my dad, who had died a year prior. He was sitting at the end of the bed in midair with his legs crossed and arms loosely crossed on his knee, which was a familiar stance for Dad. There wasn't a chair, high stool, or piece of furniture to sit on in the room, and especially at eye level. There was light shining on the left side of him and enough light around him to see him clearly. I recognized his face and the heavy Scottish brogue when he spoke.

The demon said, "Stay with him, he will take care of you." He was referring to my husband, who was a cruel, abusive, and violent man.

Even knowing in my mind that statement shouldn't be right, it would come up in my memory every time I had a new plan on how to get free from my husband. It always caused me to hesitate and question myself. I didn't believe it was really my dad, but that doubt always lingered because at that time, I didn't know anything about demons or their power.

A few weeks later, while living in that same house, my husband, unaware of what I had experienced, told me he had seen my dad sitting on the couch in the living room one night when he had come home late. The demon didn't say anything to him. It was just sitting there, smiling at him. It was so real I think it scared my husband.

My son and other kids that stayed with us had bedrooms upstairs in that house and said they heard someone dragging chains in the rooms where they slept. This happened on numerous occasions. The kids were always afraid to stay in that house and especially upstairs alone.

The Bible clearly says we as born-again children of God have authority over evil spirits. Unfortunately, at this point, I wasn't aware of what the Bible said.

> *Jesus summoned His twelve disciples and gave them authority over unclean spirits, to cast them out, and to heal every disease and every sickness. (Matthew 10:1 NASB)*

B.   Demons in the Texas House

After we moved into the house in Texas in 1994, I became aware of negative spirits in one room. Someone had been playing an evil board game or doing something in that room they shouldn't have been doing and invited evil spirits in. That just happened to be the room my daughter had chosen for her bedroom. If I could have talked her into moving to another room, I would have just shut the door and avoided using that room. But she was set on using that specific room.

Within days of moving in and getting my daughter's bedroom set up, she would cry out for me at night. She said there were things under her bed or in the corner. I would have thought it was normal childhood fears, but the hair on my arms and the back of my neck would stand on end when I stepped through the doorway, and

I knew there were spirits in the room. Since I had already learned Jesus gave us authority over spirits, I started ordering them out of my house. It took a few nighttime trips to that room, but they left. I could sense the peace in the room once they were gone.

The spirits didn't like being ejected, and they retaliated. This was something I hadn't encountered before. It took a few days to realize the physical problems that were erupting in my body were being caused by the demons.

I started having joint pain in my knees and then elbows. Then it would jump to my hip or wrist. The condition kept getting worse. I knew it was an evil spirit(s) because I could hear it laughing (through my spirit).

It would wake me at night and keep me from resting. One night, I woke up like someone had thrown a bucket of cold water on me. My whole body was dripping, the sheets and blanket were soaked, and I could barely roll out of the bed onto my hands and knees on the floor. My hair was dripping like I had just gotten out of the shower.

After that, red blood blotches started popping up on my skin— first on my left forearm, and then it would jump to my right hand. They were like liver spots that kept moving from place to place. After a couple of weeks of this continual evil abuse, my husband took me to a doctor.

That doctor just looked at me and ordered me directly to the hospital. I refused to go, and he pressured my husband by saying if he didn't make me go, he would wake up next to a corpse in the morning. The doctor's opinion was that I was so run-down I wouldn't make it through the night.

Naturally, true to my nature, I still refused to go to the hospital. But the next morning, when I wasn't any better, I agreed. The emergency room at the hospital had six to eight different doctors checking me to see if they could find the source of the ailments. Finally, after many hours and tests, they gave me a prescription of steroids and sent me home to die.

The turning point happened when I heard Gloria Copeland on TV teaching on healing. I agreed with her and claimed it. I slowly started getting better after that. From start to finish, six weeks had passed. When it ended, I was fine, and my house was clean of evil spirits.

I knew what I was fighting and knew they didn't have the authority to kill me without my agreement. However, I did learn a lesson in how much they can affect your body and the need to keep standing on the Word of God and fighting. They don't always just *flee* instantly when you tell them to.

> *Submit therefore to God. Resist the devil and*
> *he will flee from you. (James 4:7 NASB 1995)*

The stronger your witness, the bigger the problems the devil will send to distract you from sharing the good news with other people. It is important to learn your authority over the devil. When you walk in your authority and exert that authority over him, he has to back off, back down, leave—"flee from you." Just remember, there may be some time lapse in there but keep going. Don't quit until he is gone! A little bullheadedness can be an advantage in these situations.

C. Deliverance

God taught me about deliverance from evil spirits in October 1984. Even though I committed my life to the Lord on June 16, 1978, I was still smoking and totally unable to quit even for a day. It was frustrating because I wanted to fit in with the Christian people, and yet all the time, the guilt of smoking let me know I didn't.

I had smoked a pack a day for almost thirty years. It was no longer a habit. It was an addiction, and I was not in control. I had tried many times to quit, to no avail. The spirit behind those cigarettes was in control and wasn't about to let me just stop. It was easier for me to go days without food than it was to go a few hours without a cigarette.

Then one day, I was listening to a Kenneth Copeland teaching tape, and at the end during closing prayer, he said, "Someone is being delivered from smoking." I just said, "Lord, if that is true, let it be me."

When I opened my eyes, I knew I no longer needed the cigarette that was sitting there burning in the ashtray. I was free to put it out. So I did! I was so totally overjoyed I was ecstatic for weeks.

I would light a cigarette just so I could put it out, then light it again, and put it out. I was *free*! I was in control! I was on a major power trip! It was joy comparable to someone handing you $100,000,000! I wasn't thinking the situation through. I was just throwing that power around everywhere, like a kid cut loose in a candy shop. No comprehension whatsoever about the potential consequences.

This is also a good place to point out why God doesn't just give us His power to use on this earth at will. Why we need to gain some spiritual maturity to know how to handle spiritual power. Except for God's grace for a very foolish child, I could have ended up far worse off than when I started.

Finally, my friend/mentor, Vivian, told me I needed to stop flaunting around my power over cigarettes. She said I was playing with the devil and that he would snag me if I kept it up. So in January, I quit playing around, rubbing the devil's nose in it, and didn't light another one after that.

This situation made me realize there really is a devil and the bondage he can hold over people and how easy God can break that bondage when it is the right time.

It also made me realize I had been with the Lord for six years, praying most of the time to break the smoking habit, and God didn't do anything about it. From my perspective at the time, I was a good person and just needed to quit smoking to be that "perfect" Christian.

However, for those six years, God just kept talking to me about attitudes, pointing things out to me about how I responded to people, what I said, the way I said it, or what I thought about situations and about people. For six years, what was going on inside of me, inside my head, wrong ideas and beliefs, were more important to God than whether I was smoking or not. He may not have liked the smoking but He disliked the angry, defensive, belittling, disrespectful attitudes even more.

On the outside, I could look and act like anyone else. I didn't have tattoos, rebellious clothing, or hair designs. But Christians were judging and rejecting me instantly because of the smoking. God wasn't.

> *For I know that this will turn out for my deliverance through your prayers and the provision of the Spirit of Jesus Christ. (Philippians 1:19 NASB)*

> *Therefore, there is now no condemnation for those who are in Christ Jesus. For the law of the Spirit of life in Christ Jesus has set you free from the law of sin and of death. (Romans 8:1–2 NASB 1995)*

How I Learned What Heaven Is Like

John's Homecoming

When my son went home to be with the Lord on June 25, 2018, it was very important to me to really know he was in heaven. God was gracious, and one morning, after the funeral was over, everything had been done, and I had returned home to Oklahoma, I had a vision of John in heaven.

The thing that caught my attention, aside from the peace I felt from knowing he was with the Lord in heaven, was his appearance. He was an adult, young, but he didn't look as he had on this earth. I knew it was him. But what I saw, I believe, was the person God had always intended him to be.

When God created us in our mother's womb, He had a plan for our life. He had a dream of perfection for us. Yes, He knew how we would stray and what was going to happen while we are on this earth. But that didn't change His perfect dream and desire for our life.

When I saw John in heaven, I believe I was seeing God's perfect version of him, the person he was always intended to be.

I found great peace in the realization that when we are a born-again Christian, no matter how much we mess up on this earth, once we arrive in heaven, it will all be wiped away and we will finally be the best version of ourselves we could ever be and it will last for eternity.

For now we see in a mirror dimly, but then
face to face; now I know in part, but then I will

know fully, just as I also have been fully known. (1 Corinthians 13:12 NASB)

> *Enter through the narrow gate; for the gate is wide and the way is broad that leads to destruction, and there are many who enter through it. For the gate is narrow and the way is constricted that leads to life, and there are few who find it. (Matthew 7:13–14 NASB)*

There are lots of ways to go the wrong direction and one way to righteousness. Jesus is the narrow gate.

Behavior should be a reflection of the heart, but it isn't always so. Sometimes people are in a training period or a growing stage. They are in the process of behavioral changes.

God knows the truth about each person. He knows their heart. God judges hearts, not behaviors.

God's overall plan can be beyond our understanding. Jesus learned from his suffering. We also learn from ours. Just because the behavior is wrong doesn't mean the heart is.

I had to learn to put my *full* trust in God and let go of the crutches. That didn't happen overnight. It took many years. But all of those years while I was learning, I belonged to the Lord. We never *arrive* until we get to heaven, like John did.

How I Learned to Praise God

In the Sanctuary

The Bible says in many places, we are to praise God—in the sanctuary, at home, everywhere. But what does that mean?

To me, praise needs to come from my heart—a sincere heart connection saying "Thank you," "I love you," "You are wonderful." For a shy person, it can be difficult to step out and do so in a congregation of strangers.

Because people were intimidating to me, I would close my eyes at the beginning of the worship service at church and concentrate on Jesus. I see us—Jesus and me—alone and I listen to the music. If the pressure of religion around me is strong, I picture myself inside a big cardboard box so no one can see when I raise my hands or dance or sing to the Lord.

I have always chosen to sit close to the front in a sanctuary so I can imagine all the people behind me having their eyes closed and lost in their own world of worship and concentration on Jesus. This helps me put the concern for people out of my mind. Also, most of the people on the front rows actually are in their own world of worship and not paying attention to those around them, so their behavior is an encouragement that I am not alone in worship.

My conscious, logical, human mind may know everyone in the sanctuary isn't engaged, but I don't allow my thoughts to dwell on that. I do everything I can to block out the knowledge of the people around me or what they are or are not doing.

I am aware this has made me appear *odd* at times, but my relationship with Jesus is far more important to me than fitting in with people. And if it is what He wants, then it is up to me to find a way to be obedient and do what pleases Him.

Praise the Lord!

> *Praise God in His sanctuary; Praise Him in His mighty expanse. Praise Him for His mighty deeds; Praise Him according to His excellent greatness. Praise Him with trumpet sound; Praise Him with harp and lyre. Praise Him with tambourine and dancing; Praise Him with stringed instruments and flute. Praise Him with loud cymbals; Praise Him with resounding cymbals. Everything that has breath shall praise the Lord. Praise the Lord! (Psalm 150 NASB)*

FINAL THOUGHTS

*Always giving thanks **for** all things in the name
of our Lord Jesus Christ to God, even the Father.
(Ephesians 5:20 NASB 1995; emphasis mine)*

This verse is hard to accept because it says **for** all things.

Because of the life I had, when I came to the Lord, I wasn't willing to accept anything less than a true relationship with a God that could make changes in the miserable existence I found myself living. Thanking Him for saving me was easy, but thanking Him for all I went through took time.

I can be thankful what happened brought me to where I am. I can be thankful God was with me through it all and watching over me. I can thank God and not blame Him.

I can thank Him because without all that trouble, I would not have been so set on finding the relationship where I could learn and grow and have a life that is blessed, healed, prosperous, and never alone.

Look at your story through the eyes of thankfulness. No life is perfect and without problems. So own your life and be thankful God is always there, ready to take bad situations and make something good come out of it.

I used to put people that had a wonderful family and wonderful childhood on a pedestal. It was the perfect dream to me. But not now. For me, I wouldn't have the relationship I do with Jesus without the lonely, alone, insecure life I lived. And that relationship with

Jesus is worth so very much more than all the treasures and pleasures of this world or the comfort of other people.

> *Be cheerful no matter what; pray all the time; thank God no matter what happens. This is the way God wants you who belong to Christ Jesus to live. (1 Thessalonians 5:18 MSG)*

> *But a natural person does not accept the things of the Spirit of God, for they are foolishness to him; and he cannot understand them, because they are spiritually discerned. But the one who is spiritual discerns all things, yet he himself is discerned by no one. For WHO HAS KNOWN THE MIND OF THE LORD, THAT HE WILL INSTRUCT HIM? But we have the mind of Christ. (I Corinthians 2:14– 16 NASB)*

These verses communicate to me we will understand more as we get rid of anger, envy, strife, gossip, and any other ungodly behaviors. The less of the bad filling our human tank, the more good will take its place. More understanding, more wisdom, more blessing from the Lord. The more we will be able to please Him.

BIOGRAPHY

I was born on January 3, 1945, into a family unplanned. It had been seven years since their only son had been born, and they weren't expecting more children. World War II was still in full swing, though it would be ending later that year and the troops would start coming home. Families had been on rationing, and women were working in factories to help support their family, the war effort, and replace the men that were gone. Life was not easy for most families.

My father was born and raised in Scotland and came to the USA in 1926 when he was twenty-two years old. He never talked about his family or why he immigrated, though he was proud of having gone through the immigration process and becoming an American citizen. His lifestyle was based on the way he had been raised. In Scotland at that time, the fathers worked and supported their family, and any extra money was theirs to spend at the local pub or however they saw fit. The man was the head of the family both in responsibility and authority. By the time I came along, my dad was well established in spending his extra money at the local pub on a daily basis.

My mother had dreamed of having five children, however; after dealing with my brother for a few years, she abandoned that dream. My brother was a redheaded Dennis the Menace. If there was a prank to be had, Davy was either in the middle of it or the brains behind his companions' exploits. He attracted playmates like flies to honey and could always be found leading the pack. *The Little Rascals* was a show about a ragtag group of kids that were always in trouble. The program aired on the radio and later on TV. It was a popular show in that day and maybe where my brother got some of his ideas.

When I was three years old, we moved out of the city to a five-acre farm. My mother's thought was that country living would be good for her son. It would get him out of the city and into the fresh air where he hopefully wouldn't get into so much trouble. Also, there would be so much work to do with the animals, garden, and home construction her husband wouldn't have time for the local pub. Alas, neither plan worked.

My brother quickly found new friends and new adventures. My father helped finish building the farmhouse and then resumed his daily habit of spending his time at the local bar. Over the next four years, his alcohol addiction grew to the point that my mother learned how to drive a car and then moved out.

She found a live-in housekeeping position and took my brother to live with her. They had a very nice place to stay, and Davy was able to start high school in a more upper-class school district.

That left my father and me at the farm. Dad's addiction kept him at the bar anytime he wasn't working. During the hours of 9:00 a.m. to 2:00 a.m. Monday to Saturday, my dad was either at work or at the bar. He only came home to sleep (after 2:00 a.m. and before 9:00 a.m.). On Sunday, when the bar was closed, he sat with a case of beer in front of the television and didn't want to be disturbed.

On Saturdays, when he didn't have to go to work, Dad would say we were going shopping, but we never made it past the bar. I would sit at a table by myself from 9:00 a.m. to 9:00 p.m. while Dad was the life of the party, telling stories and jokes up at the bar. At 9:00 p.m., due to curfew, I had to go sit in the car until 2:00 a.m. when the bar closed.

Even at seven years old, it didn't take long for me to learn on Saturday mornings to get up early, run out into the fields, and hide. I knew Dad wouldn't look for me very long before he would leave for the bar. Nothing was important enough to be late for their 9:00 a.m. opening.

The one mistake my mother made was taking me to visit her new home and family. I spent all day watching her. In the morning, she and the lady of the house both pampered and poured love and kisses over the young master of the house as he sat at the breakfast table in his fancy little suit and bow tie, both women just gushing over him. You would have thought he was royalty or something instead of just a sick kid.

In the afternoon, we were walking to the drugstore for ice cream when the cure to my problem came to me. After all, this kid now had two moms, and I had none. In addition to that, my mother had never gushed over me for any reason, sick or not. My brilliant seven-year-old cure for that problem was to shove him off the sidewalk into oncoming traffic. Fortunately for him, my mother was holding his hand. I learned that day what anger is. My anger toward the kid and the parents shocked anger toward me. Needless to say, I was never invited back.

As a result of the family arrangement, I virtually lived alone for two years until the divorce was final. I got up alone, went to school alone, came home to an empty cold house, and went to bed when it got dark.

The hardest part was learning how to tell time so I would know when to go outside to catch the school bus. The bus driver started beeping her horn for me, which helped. I got plenty of lectures about being outside before she came until I finally figured the clock out.

I regularly forgot to comb my hair, brush my teeth, wash my face, and take any lunch. Fortunately, the school passed out milk at lunchtime in those days. At seven years old, taking baths or wearing clean clothes and matching socks weren't at all items on my priority list. I figured out how to do things when I got in trouble at school for not doing them. I was in first and second grades during this time.

When I got tired of eating whatever cold food I could find, I ventured to learning how to make the toaster work. It was an old-fashioned toaster where the sides lay down, and you put the bread in and you decided when to take it out. It didn't have a timer and pop-up like today's toasters do. I ate plenty of black bread during that learning curve.

Then I progressed on to mastering the handheld can opener and getting food out of a can. That took some work because my hands weren't strong enough to clamp the handles together. Eventually I figured out the stove and would make tomato soup and toast (brown, not black) to eat. I was living big!

A seven-year-old (even a smart one!) isn't the best to be given free rein in the kitchen. I would forget to turn the stove off and burn up my share of tomato soup pans and start a few fires. By God's grace, the fires didn't spread and just burned themselves out.

Winter in Michigan required the use of the coal furnace in the basement. The coal furnace needed a shovel or two full of coal added a few times a day to keep the fire going. In the beginning, the shovel was too big for me to pick up, so I just threw coal nuggets into the furnace through the open door. There was a time or two that old coal furnace was thumping and groaning from the inferno I had created inside it. It was really nice and summertime hot upstairs, though. It was God's grace again that I didn't cause an explosion or burn the house down.

When my parents' divorce was final, I was nine years old. Mom moved back in, and Dad left. Mom took a job at the local grocery store working noon to 9:00 p.m. She could have taken a day-shift job but she liked the manager better on the late shift. As a result, my life didn't change much. I continued to grow up very alone, lonely, and insecure.

Mom would get up to see me off to school, but I still came home after school to an empty, cold house. I was in third grade at school now and was supposed to be in bed asleep before she got home at night. One change was that Mom was picky about the way I combed my hair, brushed my teeth, washed my face, and the clothes I wore, which I am sure the teachers appreciated.

School was a haven for me. Because I was fully grown by the time I was ten years old (five feet and four inches), I towered over the other kids (including the boys) and never felt I could fit in with the other students.

However, I totally enjoyed numbers and found some personal value in getting A's. B's were okay, but they were not my goal. I gained confidence that I wasn't dumb. I won the school checker championship in fifth grade and placed third in the school district in the spelling bee when I was in eighth grade. I could learn—that was the one thing about myself that I could hold onto. I looked up to character traits like integrity, honesty, intelligence, and bravery. My superheroes were *The Adventures of Ozzie and Harriet, Father Knows Best*, and (the original) Superman!

At ten years old, I traded sucking my thumb in on a pack of cigarettes for comfort. I don't remember how young I was when I started emptying beer bottles and tasting whiskeys. I was looking for love and acceptance from anyone that would acknowledge my existence. I never had much luck finding it, though.

Mom was a pretty, small-built, five-foot-two redhead that liked to socialize and captivate the male attention. She made friends easily and liked doing things away from home. She helped farmer friends and joined a bowling league for recreation.

My dad was one of those males that kept hanging around, and after five years, they ended up getting remarried. Dad had gone "on the wagon" of nonalcohol for six months to convince her he was the man she was looking for. Those six months were great. We would go out to dinner on Friday nights and even go to the drive-in show like a real family.

Like all dreams, it came to an end when my mom insisted on having their remarriage celebration at the local bar with a bottle of champagne. She was the center of attention, but it was more than my dad's alcoholism could resist.

Being left alone so much, I longed for the perfect family—*The Adventures of Ozzie and Harriet* and *Father Knows Best* became my fantasy family. In my mind, all I had to do was grow up, get married, and live happily ever after, or so the dream went.

I was a good student in school but the full scholarship to college didn't interest me at all. My total focus was on my dream family. The fact that I was forcibly raped at thirteen years old and then became a teenage alcoholic didn't change the dream.

My first marriage was at seventeen years old, midway through my senior high school year. I had met and latched onto Johnny when I was fourteen. He had a family! They had Sunday dinners together, went on picnics, played badminton in the backyard, and cared about each other. I was totally sold on that being my dream family. I went to their house as often as I could and longed to be invited to those Sunday dinners. That was heaven to me. I wanted to be a part of that family so much I overlooked and excused everything Johnny did that showed he had no real care for me.

We married when I was seventeen, but the dream never got any further than my head. He was nineteen years old, in the military at the time stationed in Germany, and used marrying me to get himself out of a shotgun wedding with a very irate German father. There was never any real semblance of togetherness beyond a signed piece of paper. We only lived together, off and on, for a total of ten months out of five years of marriage.

The last "reunion" only lasted until I got pregnant with my son. That was the straw that broke the camel's back. By this time, he was stationed outside of Washington DC. He convinced me to sell my car and then he moved back to the army base and abandoned me, leaving me living too far from anything to survive without begging someone for a ride.

He left me alone in a run-down apartment building with no heat or air-conditioning and with bats living in the walls. You couldn't open the windows in the hot weather without the house filling with black bats flying at my head. The closest phone was three flights down and a block down the street to a pay phone. Without a car, I had to beg fellow workers for a ride to and from my place of employment. Without a car, I wasn't able to get food, maternity clothes, or see a doctor. The mail was only available on Saturday mornings in this one-block-long, out-of-the-way country town. At nine months pregnant, I realized I had to face facts, call my mother for help, and go home where I could get medical treatment to help with the birth. I was twenty years old.

Back at the family farm, my son was born, and I got a job and became buried in all the routine work of taking care of a baby. At that time, we used cloth diapers that had to be handwashed daily before going to the laundromat for machine washing. Formula was made each evening for the next day, and my ailing father also needed daily meal care. I was developing a Cinderella complex with the all-work-and-no-play lifestyle I found myself in.

My dad's health had already started deteriorating before I moved back home. There were numerous problems that had caused him to quit working, and he would spend months at a time in the hospitals until he died on July 31, 1967, when I was twenty-two years old. Three years later, my mother remarried, sold the family farm, and moved to Florida.

I believe most people instinctively are doing the best they can in the circumstances in which they find themselves. My dad, in a foreign land away from immediate family, clung to the lifestyle he knew as a child. My mother found herself married to a good provider but also an alcoholic. She had a son going without that needed father's close attention and direction and a daughter that was exceptionally quiet, withdrawn, and could be easily forgotten. As a result, my mother turned to outside friends for solace, as did my brother.

Like all good stories, a few months before my dad passed on and when I was feeling a lot like Cinderella, a Knight in Shining Armor showed up to presumably rescue the damsel in distress out of her life of drudgery. The only problem was this Knight only shined until I said, "I do."

Slowly, over time, I found myself in a position I couldn't get out of with a man that was a violent, controlling, abusive criminal. The best way I found to describe him was that he was involved in organized criminal activity when I met him in Detroit. We moved to Indiana where he got involved with the Klu Klux Klan, and after we moved to Phoenix, he started bringing Hells Angels home to dinner.

I was told I knew too much to leave on more than one occasion. However, I had no idea what it was he thought I knew, since I wasn't a part of their activities. In his mind, he owned me. God's protective hand was on my life during those years because there were numerous times I could have/should have died but somehow didn't. I was aware of other people that had encountered him and his friends but weren't as fortunate.

It was ten long years before the devil's grip started to loosen, just a little, on my life. A ray of hope flickered and started growing. It took a year and a number of events, but I was able to get a divorce while he was gone for a number of months and I didn't know his whereabouts. This happened during the 1960s and 1970s when laws and assistance organizations were not established yet like they are now.

Two weeks later, after the divorce was final, I had the second encounter with Jesus. I was baptized in His Holy Spirit and was no longer alone or defenseless.

This is where my story really begins. My life hasn't been free of problems, and some of the worst situations I ever had to deal with happened as a Christian, but I was no longer alone and no longer the victim. Jesus made me victorious, above and not beneath, the head and not the tail. He has seen me through it all.

After many years, I eventually went on to a third marriage, convinced the past had been all my fault because I didn't trust people. So I started trusting and I trusted him completely, letting myself believe I had found the perfect Christian relationship.

After nineteen years, I found out he was truly, to me, a wolf in sheep's clothing and the worst one of them all. Even though I was a Christian when we married, there was still a great deal I didn't understand about God, His promises, and Christian relationships. The warning signs were there; I just didn't put the value to them like I needed to.

Before commitment to Jesus in a person's life, they have trouble because they are alone in this world without a Savior. After commitment to Jesus in that person's life, they have trouble because they are now an enemy of the devil, and he is afraid they will tell others about Jesus and how much He has changed their life. Trouble isn't something any of us will ever totally escape on this side of heaven.

The main things I have learned in this life since my first encounter with God at four years old are

1. to put other people before myself;
2. to respect the authority figures over me;
3. to not think too high (or too low) of myself;
4. to be thankful for life, freedom, all that I have;
5. to not be wasteful;
6. to put God first;

7. when God is first, He will bless your life with:
   a. peace, love, joy
   b. financial security
   c. accomplishments
8. God is always there, watching over; and
9. God will be my protection.

In closing, this is a summary of the major stories and issues God has taught me. It is by no means anywhere near *all* He has taught me. God doesn't teach everyone the same way or exactly the same things. He teaches each of us in a very loving, kind way according to what we need to gain a fruitful, blessed, spiritually mature life with Him.

Life with Jesus is an ongoing daily adventure. He is always there, always ready to hear, to teach, or to consult on anything I have to say, question, or comment on. The day will come when I will be able to go to heaven with Him, and it will be joy unspeakable!

> *He who dwells in the shelter of the Most High will abide in the shadow of the Almighty. I will say to the Lord, "My refuge and my fortress, My God, in whom I trust!"*
>
> *For it is He who delivers you from the snare of the trapper and from the deadly pestilence. He will cover you with His pinions, and under His wings you may seek refuge; His faithfulness is a shield and bulwark. You will not be afraid of the terror by night, or of the arrow that flies by day; of the pestilence that stalks in darkness, or of the destruction that lays waste at noon. A thousand may fall at your side and ten thousand at your right hand, but it shall not approach you. You will only look on with your eyes and see the recompense of the wicked. For you have made the Lord, my refuge, even the Most High, your dwelling place. No evil will befall you, nor will any plague come near your tent. For He will give His angels charge concerning you, to guard*

you in all your ways. They will bear you up in their hands, that you do not strike your foot against a stone. You will tread upon the lion and cobra, the young lion and the serpent you will trample down. Because he has loved Me, therefore I will deliver him: I will set him securely on high, because he has known My name. He will call upon Me, and I will answer him; I will be with him in trouble; I will rescue him and honor him. With a long life I will satisfy him and let him see My salvation. (Psalm 91 NASB 1995)

I encourage you to reread Psalm 91, changing the *you* to *me* and *He* or *I* to *Jesus*. Personalize this psalm as Jesus speaking directly to you. This exercise never fails to enhance the meaning and relationship I feel with Jesus.

Since committing my life to God in 1978, Jesus has never failed me. No matter what the situation or problem, He has always been there and always brought me through better than before. Some things took longer than others to master, but God never left me. He has provided a way when there was no way. He has blessed me when I didn't believe I was worth anything much less a blessing. He has raised me up and given me a very good life full of peace, love, joy, strength, happiness, and, most of all, friendship with Him.

ABOUT THE AUTHOR

Janet M. Sanders is a retired tax accountant and active member of the Assembly at Broken Arrow, Oklahoma. At seventy-seven years of age, Janet still has a full and active life, as her attention has turned to writing and volunteer work. She encourages faith and trust in God wherever she goes.

www.ingramcontent.com/pod-product-compliance
Lightning Source LLC
Chambersburg PA
CBHW061323120726
48001CB00002B/652